KIT HOMES

Your Guide to Home-Building Options,
from Catalogs to Factories

Rich Binsacca

The
Globe
Pequot
Press

GUILFORD, CONNECTICUT

To buy books in quantity for corporate use or incentives, call **(800) 962–0973, ext. 4551,** or e-mail **premiums@GlobePequot.com.**

Text design by Tom Goddard
Illustrations by Mary Ballachino

Library of Congress Cataloging-in-Publication Data
Binsacca, Rich.
     Kit Homes: your guide to home-building options, from catalogs to factories /
Rich Binsacca.
     p. cm.
   Includes index.
   ISBN-13: 978-0-7627-3141-1
   ISBN-10: 0-7627-3141-9
   1. House construction—Popular works. I. Title.
TH4811B56 2006
690'.837—dc22
                                                                              2006001726

Manufactured in the United States of America
First Edition/First Printing

This book is dedicated to my loving and supportive wife, Duanea, and my sons, Sam and Nick. And to Zoë, who watched it all happen and provided (mostly unsolicited) commentary.

Contents

Acknowledgments

Several people helped make this book a reality. I especially want to thank Boyce Thompson at *Builder* magazine for his recommendation. Thanks also to David Emblidge and the editorial staff at The Globe Pequot Press for their faith and exceptional work; and to the National Association of Home Builders (NAHB) Building Systems Council, the NAHB Research Center, *Automated Builder* magazine, and the Manufactured Housing Institute for access to information about the kit and manufactured home industries.

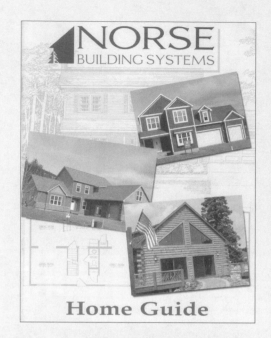

NORSE
BUILDING SYSTEMS

Home Guide

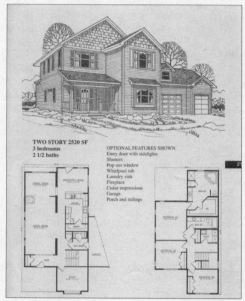

TWO STORY 2520 SF
3 bedrooms
2 1/2 baths

OPTIONAL FEATURES SHOWN:
Entry door with sidelights
Shutters
Pop out window
Whirlpool tub
Laundry sink
Fireplace
Cedar impressions
Garage
Porch and railings

Introduction

Welcome to the world of kit homes.

Like any good companion, this book is at your side to offer advice and guidance, provide essential tools, suggest additional resources, and—if you need it—hold your hand (so to speak) through the process of planning for and purchasing a kit home.

For the purposes of giving you a broad perspective of your options, *Kit Homes* defines "kit" homes as those derived from newsstand, mail-order, and online catalogs (as well as house plans from those sources, which can be used to purchase materials for their construction) and manufactured homes and derivatives of factory-built (or prefab) housing. To help discern the difference and speed your learning curve of the lingo, there's a running, on-page glossary of terms you'll come across as you read the text, plus a complete glossary at the back of the book.

The thought behind including a wider range of housing options than traditional "kit homes," in which you order the blueprints and materials package together and assemble the house on a chosen home site, was to underscore the fact that you have several choices to achieve your housing dreams.

Kit homes, as this book defines them, offer an alternative to traditional "site" or "stick-built" homes offered by developers and home builders that have relatively few opportunities to suit your specific lifestyle needs and desires. Kit homes, whether simply a set of blueprints from a catalog or a near-complete manufactured home, can provide a higher level of design flexibility, cost and time efficiencies, and location choices for your particular circumstances.

To get you up to speed on how these different forms of kit homes emerged and have evolved through our nation's history, this book provides a brief history of both the catalog and manufactured home industries. In chapter 1 you'll gain an appreciation for the production methods and marketing savvy pioneered by Sears, Roebuck & Company's *Modern Homes* catalog (among a half-dozen peers of its day), and learn how the legacy of its approach to the market lives on in today's homes from a catalog.

A typical house from the Modern Homes *catalog offered in the first half of the twentieth century by Sears, Roebuck & Company features a simple yet classic design that appealed to the tastes and the budgets of the growing middle class and helped shape the character of early American suburbs.*

In addition, chapter 1 provides insight into the evolution of the manufactured home industry, from its roots in the pull-behind trailer coaches of the 1920s to modern, multisection homes that meet strict federal standards for quality and energy efficiency.

The "Before You Build" section (chapter 2) offers a guide to the planning process that will establish a solid foundation for critical decisions about your new home. This chapter encourages and provides the tools to help you assess your lifestyle needs and wants; determine what you can afford to spend; identify various options to finance your project; calculate and anticipate costs for design, construction, and maintenance; and define your role as the home owner and leader of the kit home journey.

With a foundation for decision making in place, the next two chapters define and detail your two basic kit home options: "Homes from a Catalog" (chapter 3) and "Homes from a Factory" (chapter 4). Both chapters delve into specifics about your choices, from ordering house plans from a Web site or printed catalog to be used for a materials purchase to ordering complete house kits (chapter 3), and the ever-expanding options afforded by factory-built manufactured and modular homes.

In both chapters you'll learn about the design process for all of the options at your disposal, such as how to make changes to a "stock" house or kit home plan before ordering materials and finishes, and the costs associated with requesting such changes. The two chapters include advice about selecting a contractor to help build or manage the project. Both offer helpful pros and cons synopses for quick reference.

If you've never seen how a kit or manufactured home goes together, chapters 3 and 4 take you step-by-step, in both narrative text and sequential photos, through their respective building processes. And while it is truly eye-opening to follow the on-site assembly of a kit home's materials or the assembly-line process of a manufactured home factory through a series of photos—insight that home owners rarely get—it will be even more dramatic when you follow your own home's building progress.

"Homes from a Catalog" also provides details about building options within its realm, including roof trusses, wall panels, and other components that speed the construction process, cut costs, and deliver a higher level of design flexibility and overall quality. You'll learn what's included in a typical kit home package and what needs to be done to finish the house before you move in.

Similarly, chapter 4 offers detailed insight into manufactured and modular homes—including the critical differences between these two types of factory-built housing options—that will help you decide if homes from a factory are the right decision for your needs. You'll learn about the U.S. Department of Housing and Urban Development (HUD) code that has regulated manufactured housing since the mid-1970s, how and why these homes are sold through networks of local and regional dealer-builders, and what you can expect from a manufacturer and its local dealer representative in terms of services and warranties.

In addition to the meat found in chapters 3 and 4, each one provides its own catalog in the form of comprehensive directories to house plan and kit home publishers and suppliers, and to manufactured and modular home producers, respectively. Use these guides to find and research sources and narrow your choices among kit home providers as you work through the planning and purchasing process.

The book also features handy worksheets to help you calculate financial affordability, determine and prioritize your wants and needs for a new home, and outline the up-front and ongoing costs of designing, building, and maintaining a home. Blank worksheets are provided in the back of the book for your use.

Kit Homes is a follow-up to *How to Afford Your Own Log Home* by Carl Heldmann, originally published by Globe Pequot in 1984 and currently in its fifth edition. *How to Afford Your Own Log Home* focuses on the log home industry, which is almost exclusively served by kit home pack-

Similar to the packaged home kits offered by Sears and others, today's modular homes are among several building systems that offer affordability and efficient construction in styles that are indistinguishable from traditional stick-built homes.

Regardless of which path you take to create your new home, a successful project always includes effective communication with design and building professionals.

ages available from printed, mail-order, and Internet-based catalogs and suppliers. In 2003 Lyons Press published *The Timberframe Way* by Michael Morris and Dick Pirozzolo, which spotlights post-and-beam construction methods and materials, of which modern versions are often provided as kit home packages as well. You might find these books interesting, along with the other titles listed in the recommended reading section at the back of this book.

On behalf of everyone involved in the design and production of *Kit Homes,* I hope you find this book a valuable resource that lives up to its name and helps deliver a successful and satisfying home-buying experience.

CHAPTER 1

Kit Home History

ON THE OUTSKIRTS OF WASHINGTON, D.C., is a neighborhood of homes built during the 1920s. Each wood-framed, clapboard-sided home sits on its own half acre along tree-lined streets with no sidewalks, fronting small, detached garages built thirty years later when cars became a popular necessity.

Inside the three-bedroom, one-bath homes are the simple yet elegant characteristics of their time: pine or oak floors, carved wood support columns, and staircases—most of which are now stripped of the carpet or paint that exemplified wealth back then. People of adequate means in the first quarter of the twentieth century preferred to cover the bare wood elements of their homes rather than expose them, unwittingly setting the stage for an industry of paint stripping and wood floor refinishing methods and materials two generations later.

As seen in this photo from a 1920 employee magazine from Standard Oil (Indiana), kit homes were the backbone of company-town housing during the height of the Industrial Revolution, representing the first residential construction boom in U.S. history.

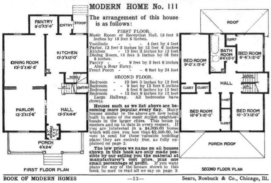

Sears pioneered the home plan publishing business with its Modern Homes *and other catalogs; not much has changed since then— except, of course, the price.*

Floor plan: The interior layout of a house, usually shown in two-dimensional format from a bird's-eye view.

Blueprints: The detailed plans used to gain approvals and for construction; also known as "working drawings" or "construction drawings."

Precut: Structural lumber and components that prior to delivery have been cut to length or to fit according to the plans and specifications.

Though the look of these one-family homes resembles the general style and construction of those built in similar communities a few decades earlier, before the turn of the last century, they represent a milestone in American housing: the initial advent of homes for the masses. Flush from the early returns of the Industrial Revolution, the families of the country's emerging middle class had, for the first time, the financial ability to afford their own homes . . . and many had the skills to build them.

What they lacked, however, were the means to hire an architect to design their family home. Though local carpenters and builders followed similar *floor plans* and materials dimensions for the homes they built, each new house required an original set of plans—an impractical requirement for a middle class that was less concerned about making an architectural statement than owning a slice of the American dream. Besides, designers of the day tended to focus instead on stately manors for business and political leaders.

In addition, these new home buyers lacked an adequate local supply of ready-to-build materials. Lumber mills then were set up to handle one or two homes at a time—the pace set by the previous generation—and simply were unable to keep up with the growing demand.

A handful of entrepreneurial companies, chief among them Sears, Roebuck & Company, took advantage of the void between design and materials supply and public demand by offering predesigned and packaged—or kit—homes from mail-order catalogs.

Sears issued its first *Modern Homes* catalog in 1908, including more than forty house designs and accompanying materials packages priced as low as $600 (about $9,000 today). The company credited the one-dollar cost for *blueprints* toward the purchase of a 30-ton delivery of *precut* materials needed for a home's complete construction, which was delivered along the rail systems from the company's network of regional lumber mills, factories, and warehouses managed from its Chicago headquarters.

The kits provided families with the quality housing designs and materials they demanded at an affordable price and in a timely manner: A month or so after ordering by mail, you'd be notified to pick up a package of cut-to-size (precut) lumber—

plus every nail, shingle, and stair part you'd need—at the nearest train station, haul it to your half-acre site, and start building.

By the mid-1920s Sears alone sold 200 or more homes a month from catalogs boasting nearly 400 different designs to accommodate a variety of regional styles and tastes and resulting in annual sales of $10 million or more. At the time, Sears and its contemporaries also offered *private financing* (as well as furniture and appliances, in Sears's case), acting as a bank to enable families to receive, build, and move into their new homes on credit.

On the one hand, offering loans expanded the realm of people who could purchase a *kit home* from Sears; on the other, it put the company at financial risk to collect monthly payments. As the Great Depression swept the 1930s, collecting became futile. In 1934 Sears liquidated about $11 million in defaulted mortgage loans. Sales never recovered, and the company sold its last kit home in 1940.

Though Sears is the best known and most prolific among the mail-order home companies of its day, with an estimated 75,000 homes sold in the program's thirty-two-year history, others survived into the second half of the twentieth century to supply the next milestone in American housing: the *baby boom generation* of the post–World War II era.

Aladdin Homes, for instance, began selling homes from a catalog in 1906 to capture a market for small summer vacation cottages, among other sideline structures and *outbuildings* for farm families and suburbanites, and the company survived the Depression to continue sales of kit homes well into the second half of the century.

Based in Bay City, Michigan, Aladdin Homes pioneered the concept of selling home plans and materials packages of similar styles and sizes to developers to create entire neighborhoods and so-called company towns, especially near the company's Rust Belt roots.

Towns such as Flint, Michigan, and Brady's Bend, Pennsylvania, emerged to support the automotive, iron, steel, textile, timber, and coal industries across the country. As factory owners began to locate their facilities closer to resources and away from urban areas (and a built-in workforce), they recognized the need to move homes to the workplace.

Aladdin, Sears, and others offered regional variations of house types, such as box bungalows in the South and Southwest and gabled frame homes in the North and East, varying in price from $600 for a two-room home with no indoor plumbing to perhaps $1,500 or more for a four-room, modern home.

Private financing: Lending services or loans offered by the builder; also known as "in-house financing."

Kit home: A package of building materials based on a selected floor plan and specifications from a single supplier or manufacturer.

Baby boom generation: Roughly the generation of American citizens born between 1946 and 1964, representing about 80 million people.

Outbuildings: Separate or supplemental structures from the house or main building on the same property.

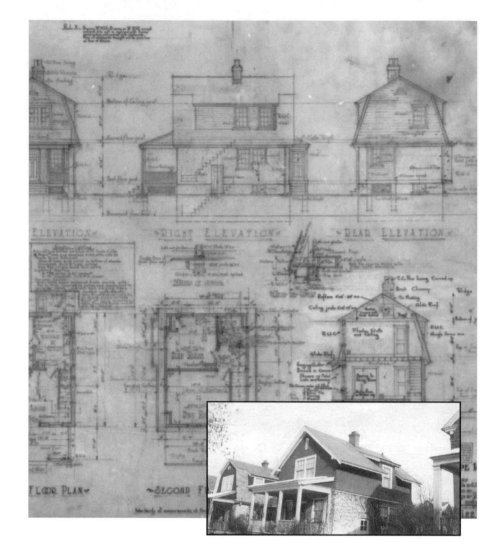

Large industrial employers, from automakers to steel and lumber mills, leveraged the cost-efficient benefits of mail-order kit homes to build modest yet modern homes and neighborhoods for their employees.

The concept is still marketed among today's home plan publishers and kit home suppliers to help quickly develop communities along a city's fringes as well as resort towns along every coast and in the shadows of mountain ranges throughout the country.

Kit home buyers of the 1920s were a lot like you: anxious for a family or vacation home on a budget, in a style that complemented regional tastes while providing some measure of distinction, such as a slightly different roofline or exterior finish. Though perhaps more skilled at actually constructing their kit homes than most folks today, they appreciated the same affordability and ease of construction that Sears and its peers provided—a legacy that survives among twenty-first-century kit home providers.

It's likely that this suburban house was constructed using a variety of industrial or factory-built structural components, or perhaps even a modular building system, as opposed to traditional stick-framing methods . . . and that its floor plan was selected from a catalog offered by the builder or house plan publisher.

Early mail-order homes weren't the only housing innovation of the early twentieth century. America's burgeoning personal wealth, combined with a newfound mobility offered by an emerging interstate highway system, fostered the development of the trailer coach. Pulled behind beefy sedans, these two-wheeled mobile homes enabled folks to visit the nation's newly created national park system or take a seasonal respite in comfort and convenience.

By the 1950s, trailer coaches had become more sophisticated mobile homes, complete with bathrooms and more extensive cooking facilities instead of simple sleeping quarters—in a growing number of cases serving as primary or at least seasonal residences as well as temporary housing for returning GIs. Recognizing the trend, and its hazards, in the 1970s the federal government began regulating the largest and increasingly less-mobile segment of the mobile homes as housing instead of recreational vehicles.

By the 1940s and '50s, trailer coaches were modern homes on wheels, providing temporary shelter for an increasingly mobile public.

Mobile home parks, like this one for returning military personnel attending the University of Missouri–Columbia on the G.I. bill following World War II, evolved into more permanent housing communities, with more permanent (if still "mobile") homes.

Chassis: A metal frame with wheels and a tow bar upon which manufactured (HUD-code) homes are built, enabling them to be towed by big rig from the factory to the home site.

Placed: A manufactured home craned into place on its foundation or pad at the home site; also known as "set."

Since then, what began as trailer coaches in the 1920s splintered into three distinct factions. The closest to the root in today's context are trailer campers, also called "fifth wheels," pulled behind pickup trucks and SUVs to serve as temporary housing during family camping trips, hunting and fishing excursions, and other recreational ventures.

Recreational vehicles, or RVs or mobile homes, are the next step up, combining the truck and trailer into one vehicle. Though serving a similar purpose of mobile, temporary living quarters as a fifth-wheel trailer, RVs offer more extensive conveniences that attract people with the time to make long interstate journeys and seasonal relocations (think retired couples escaping to Arizona from their Minnesota home in the winter), replacing airports and motel rooms with cushy, homelike settings that travel with them.

The third faction of the trailer-coach era is the manufactured home—the one of the three that's considered (and regulated) by the government as housing instead of vehicle. Though built on a *chassis* for transportation by big rig that remains as its foundation, a manufactured home is rarely moved once it is *placed* on a plot of land.

Modern fifth-wheel trailers are the most direct spin-off from the trailer coaches of the 1920s, providing their owners with pull-behind, temporary housing that features several conveniences.

The evolved trailer coach is the recreational vehicle, or RV, which is more accurately a mobile home compared to today's manufactured (or HUD-code) housing. Both RVs and fifth-wheels (pictured above) are regulated as vehicles, while manufactured homes are considered housing.

Outfitted like any home, complete with walled bedrooms, full bathrooms, comfortable living areas, and modern kitchens, manufactured homes have slowly evolved from their mobile roots to become legitimate alternatives to permanent *site-built* homes—with the newest versions placed on concrete foundations that truly render them immobile. For folks looking for affordable vacation homes or primary residences set in subdivisions instead of trailer parks, today's manufactured homes provide a practical solution.

Site-built: Houses built entirely on the home site (instead of in a factory).

Though several turn-of-the-twentieth-century innovations combined to help create modern home-building methods, products, and development—including the automobile, interstate highway system, indoor plumbing, and federally insured home mortgage industry—Sears, Aladdin Homes, and the first trailer-coach manufacturers played a huge role in setting the stage for mass housing production in the post–World War II era. By producing and packaging an entire home (or perhaps building the thing on wheels) in a factory, manufacturers ushered industrialization into the home-building lexicon; by making homes affordable, they opened the market to the middle class and even the working poor.

Much has changed in manufactured housing during the past thirty years, from the design and materials of the homes to where and how they are placed, finished, and enhanced by add-on features. Manufactured houses were long relegated to trailer parks (top). Today's HUD-code homes are more likely found in traditional subdivisions, where they enjoy property-value appreciation similar to site-built homes.

Prehung windows: Windows built with a frame and sill that are preassembled in a factory and installed as is during construction.

Plated roof trusses: Factory-built roof framing components, in which steel plates hold sections of lumber together in a designed pattern or shape.

The factory technology to provide a package of precut lumber and other building materials (in the case of kit homes) or provide a near-complete house (as with manufactured homes) created or evolved into such industries as ***prehung windows*** and ***plated roof trusses,*** among a wide variety of factory-fabricated materials for home building that today support the construction of two million new homes a year and satisfy the often-conflicting demands for faster construction, lower costs, and better quality.

Sears estimated that a home from its precut lumber and complete materials package could be built 40 percent faster than a comparable house using traditional construction methods and tools. The same structure today might go up in half the time thanks to the factory-built windows, doors, siding panels, and other finishes that have evolved from those pioneering kit home packages.

While this country's industrial age through the 1940s perhaps plodded along compared to today's dynamic information age, its legacy in housing remains and continues to inspire (or at least support) those serving the needs of today's home buyers and builders.

For instance, buyers are still allowed—as they were in the '20s—to select a design and receive a load of materials from modern kit home suppliers, many of which have established a foothold in rural and resort markets as people search for getaways, weekend vacation spots, and quiet retirement locations.

Meanwhile, the concept of selecting a house plan from a catalog lives on among a sea of home plan publishers and online sources that, like the Sears *Modern Homes* catalog, offer an affordable alternative to architectural design and provide a complete list of materials that any local lumberyard today can fulfill and deliver for construction.

A modern manufactured (or HUD-code) housing factory might have a half dozen or more homes in various stages of construction at any given time.

More than 90 percent of a manufactured home is constructed under roof (or "off-site") under strict quality control and federal building codes.

Materials arrive at the job site, just as they did with kit homes of the past. In this case, the materials come in the form of pre-built wall panels that help reduce the cost and time of on-site construction.

The legacy even lives on among professional home builders, the majority of whom use at least some form of factory-built framing, such as prebuilt roof trusses, and all of whom rely on modern manufacturing capabilities for everything from roofing and siding to countertops and floor finishes.

In fact, you don't have to look very closely to follow the bloodline of the early pioneers of industrialized housing—a heritage that today enables nearly everyone to participate in home ownership.

Engineered, factory-built components, such as roof assemblies, evolved from the precut lumber packages shipped by Sears and others to reduce the time and complexity of on-site residential construction.

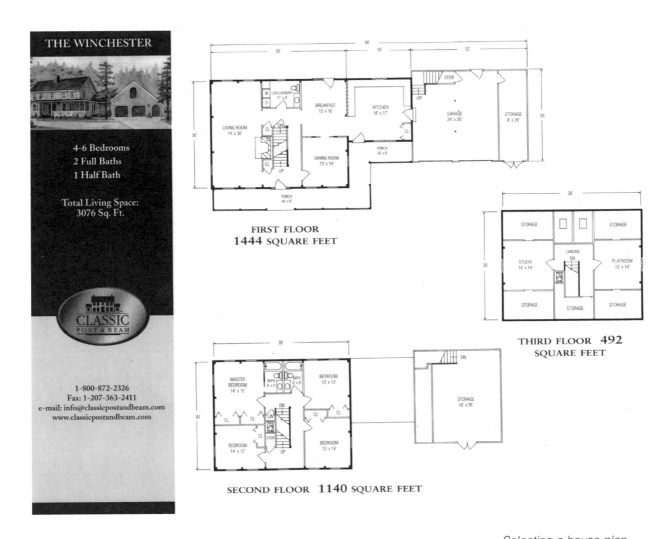

THE WINCHESTER

4-6 Bedrooms
2 Full Baths
1 Half Bath

Total Living Space:
3076 Sq. Ft.

CLASSIC
POST & BEAM

1-800-872-2326
Fax: 1-207-363-2411
e-mail: info@classicpostandbeam.com
www.classicpostandbeam.com

FIRST FLOOR
1444 SQUARE FEET

LIVING ROOM 14' x 30'
LAV/LAUNDRY 11' x 8'
BREAKFAST 13' x 16'
KITCHEN 16' x 17'
GARAGE 24' x 26'
STORAGE 8' x 26'
STOR
DINING ROOM 13' x 14'
PORCH 16' x 6'
PORCH 44' x 6'

THIRD FLOOR 492
SQUARE FEET

STORAGE
STORAGE
STUDIO 14' x 14'
LANDING DN
PLAYROOM 13' x 14'
STORAGE
STORAGE
STORAGE

SECOND FLOOR 1140 SQUARE FEET

MASTER BEDROOM 14' x 15'
BATH 5' x 9'
BATH 5' x 9'
BEDROOM 13' x 13'
BEDROOM 14' x 12'
LIN
STOR
BEDROOM 13' x 14'
DN
STORAGE 18' x 26'

Selecting a house plan from a printed or online catalog is roughly the same process as it was in the 1920s, though few publishers also sell the materials package that goes with their drawings.

CHAPTER 2

Before You Build

REGARDLESS OF WHAT TYPE of home or construction method you eventually choose, a significant amount of planning needs to occur before you break ground. Like a home's foundation, proper and thorough preparation prior to construction establishes a stable platform of expectations that will direct the rest of the process.

Adequately preparing for your new home, whether it's intended to be your primary residence or a second or vacation property, involves determining a budget and financing options, finding the place and particular *parcel* of land for your home, assessing your needs and wants, and calculating costs. The goal is to bring dreams and reality into balance—to get what you need (and, hopefully, most of what you want) at a price you can afford.

In addition to these preparatory steps, you'll want to determine your role as the home owner. For some, that means being the builder or general contractor, while others prefer a hands-off approach or somewhere between those extremes. Several factors work into determining your role in the project, but the bottom line is making a commitment to that role and setting a good example for the rest of the project team to follow.

Parcel:
Land or home site.

Getting your financial house in order, as well as your thoughts and ideas down on paper and prioritized, is an essential step before you even consider a house plan or type of construction for your new home.

13

Housing Options

This book offers home buyers two basic kit home options: homes from a catalog and homes from a factory. Within those general categories, however, are a variety of terms and options for obtaining house plans, construction and finish materials, additional cost efficiencies, and professional help. This chart outlines those terms and options and presents a useful reference that summarizes the information you'll find in the pages of *Kit Homes*.

Homes from a Catalog

Types of construction: Raw or precut materials assembled on-site
Sources of house plans: Catalog, house plan book, or Web site
Sources of labor: Home buyer, supplier, and/or contractors
Sources of materials: Kit supplier or lumberyard plus various sources for systems and finishes
Possible cost efficiencies: Use of factory-built framing components (versus stick framing)
Off-site versus on-site construction: Mostly on-site

Homes from a Factory

Types of construction: Manufactured or modular homes built and/or assembled in a factory
Sources of house plans: Supplier catalogs (printed or online)
Sources of labor: Factory workers (home); home buyer or contractors for site improvements
Sources of materials: Inclusive in home, selected by home buyer
Possible cost efficiencies: Selection of smaller home, fewer options; no extra site improvements
Off-site versus on-site construction: Up to 90 percent off-site

Key Terms

Engineered framing components: A generic term for roof trusses, wall and roof panels, and floor trusses, which are assembled/built in a factory and shipped to the job site to help speed on-site construction of major structural framing sections (e.g., the roof).

HUD code: The building codes and standards for manufactured homes established and enforced by the U.S. Department of Housing and Urban Development (HUD).

Kit home package: An unassembled package of building materials, typically raw or precut lumber and other rough framing components, for a specific house plan selected by the home buyer, delivered to the job site for assembly.

Manufactured housing: General term for homes built in a factory to federal standards set by HUD.

Modular homes: Homes primarily built in a factory in large sections, including rough mechanical systems but often lacking most finishes; assembled and finished on the job site.

Off-site: Synonymous with manufactured or HUD-code homes; a home built primarily in a factory and shipped nearly complete to the job site.

On-site: Opposite of off-site; a home built primarily on the job site using raw or precut lumber and other materials needed for completion.

There are a lot of decisions to make at this stage, some obvious and others requiring difficult trade-offs and perhaps lifestyle changes, if temporarily. Always try to keep your eye on the prize: a new home that, if you've prepared properly, will forever be a source of pride and accomplishment.

Calculating Affordability

For better or worse, money is arguably *the* driving factor in your home-building project, and creating and committing to a budget is critical to its success. In many cases, home buyers have no idea where to start in determining a budget for a house; there are so many variables and considerations that the task seems overwhelming.

The mistake people make is trying to determine *costs* instead of a budget. Rest assured, you'll get a dose of what things cost before you proceed with the project and throughout construction. For now, however, the goal is to simply figure out what you can *afford*, providing a way to match your wants and needs—and quite possibly your eventual choice of a construction process—to your available finances.

Whether or not we formally keep track, most of us work from a budget of monthly income and expenses. Therefore, determining what you can afford per month is an appropriate gauge to use, even if you have to make a **lump-sum payment** for land, design fees, or another expense at some point in the process. If you're financing all or part of your project with a loan, for instance, it'll be paid back on a monthly basis. On the flip side, what you can afford per month will factor into the amount you can borrow and how quickly you can repay it.

If you're planning to build a primary residence (that is, move into it from your current house or apartment), determining your budget is, for the most part, a tab of your existing housing expenses: monthly rent or mortgage payment, taxes and insurance, utilities and services, maintenance and improvements, and perhaps annual or ad hoc fees. Add any nonessential monthly expenses you're willing to consider.

If you're planning for a second or vacation home (from now on simply referred to as a "second home"), your monthly calculation must be *in addition* to your existing housing costs—essentially, your monthly income minus all of your required or necessary expenses, commonly called "disposable income."

Here's where trade-offs come into play. All of us spend money on nonessential items and services, such as entertainment, travel, gifts, a health club membership, charitable donations, and even walking-around cash for that occasional caffe latte or lunch out. Some folks may sock away a percentage of disposable income in a savings account or in short- or long-term investments, such as an interest-bearing money market account or retirement fund.

Lump-sum payment:
A debt or cost paid at one time instead of amortized over time.

Are you willing to sacrifice a few lattes to boost your housing affordability? Trimming relatively small (and nonessential) expenses can add up to help stretch your budget.

Before you give up your daily Starbucks, however, wrangle all of these expenses and evaluate them. Yes, it's probably more practical to sacrifice a monthly dose of decaf mochas than an IRA deposit, but it's worth the effort to thoroughly calculate and honestly prioritize where you spend your disposable income. That effort enables you to make choices that will help determine a reasonable monthly budget for your new home.

In fact, it may take a month or two to track your expenses—all of them—before you can properly evaluate them, determine what's essential and nonessential, and make some choices to free up money for a house and related project costs (covered later in this chapter).

Determining what's essential and what is not is entirely up to you, though costs for housing, food, utilities, insurance, and other basic needs might best be left off the table of consideration. That said, you may be willing to live without "essentials" such as restaurant meals, premium cable TV or Internet packages, extended service warranties, or lawn care services to boost your affordability . . . if only until you reach your goal and move into your new home. You can revisit those "essential" luxuries once you reach your goal, or you may find that you really don't miss them.

Once you have a good handle on what you spend every month for nonessential items, prioritize and segment them into those you are truly willing to sacrifice right away and those you'd rather not unless absolutely necessary. Add the items in each column (or grouping) to determine a baseline of dollars you are willing, and unwilling, to make available for your project (see the Housing Affordability Worksheet sample on the next page and the blank version of the worksheet at the back of the book).

Remember, if you're swapping primary homes instead of building a second home, consider your current housing costs—including mortgage payment or rent, insurance, property taxes, and utilities—as part of your monthly tally of available funds, at least for the purposes of selecting among various financing options explained in the next section.

Once you've completed the worksheet, congratulations; you've just figured out your affordability.

HOUSING AFFORDABILITY WORKSHEET

Determine which nonessential expenses (and perhaps some essential expenses) you are willing to sacrifice outright or reduce (and by how much) to free up funds toward a down payment, land purchase, or related expense for your new home. (For a blank Housing Affordability Worksheet, turn to the back of the book.)

Month *Jan – Mar*   **Year** *2006*

ESSENTIAL	NONESSENTIAL	EXPENSES	AMOUNT (monthly average)
✔	☐	**Mortgage** (including principal, Interest, property taxes, insurance)	*$2200-*
		Utilities	
✔	☐	Natural gas/propane	
✔	☐	Electric	*$460-*
✔	☐	Water/sewer	
✔	☐	Phone	
☐	☐	Trash/recycling	*N/A*
☐	☐	Dial-up Internet/DSL	*N/A*
☐	☐	Irrigation	*N/A*
		Cable/satellite (incl. equipment)	
☐	✔	Television	
☐	✔	Internet	*$85-*
		Insurance	
✔	☐	Health/medical	
✔	☐	Auto	*$360-*
✔	☐	Life	
☐	☐	Home (unless part of mortgage)	
☐	☐	Other (specify)	
✔	☐	**Groceries/sundries**	*$550-*
✔	☐	**Medical** (out of pocket)	*$125-*
✔	☐	**Veterinary/pet care**	
✔	☐	**Vehicle payment(s)**	*$450-*
☐	☐	**Boat/recreational vehicle payments**	*$160-*
✔	☐	**Gasoline** (for vehicles)	*N/A*
☐	✔	**Lawn service**	*$50-*
☐	✔	**Health club dues/class fees**	*$120-*
☐	✔	**Home improvement**	*$160-*
☐	✔	**Self-/mini-storage**	*$35-*
☐	✔	**Haircuts/health and beauty services**	*$80-*
☐	✔	**Gifts**	*$35-*
☐	✔	**Travel**	*$250-*
☐	✔	**Entertainment**	*$100-*
☐	✔	**Newspaper/media services**	*$18-*
		Misc./other expenses (specify)	
☐	✔	*Massage (2/mo.)*	*$90-*

Raw (land): Land that has yet to be prepared for building activity; pristine or unimproved.

Undeveloped (land): Land that has been cleared or prepared for the installation of basic utility services prior to construction.

Lender: A bank or other financial institution that lends money.

Infrastructure: Primarily refers to streets, curbs, gutters, storm-water runoff provisions, and other basic utility services necessary before construction begins.

Financing Options

The average new house today, including land, costs a hair less than $250,000. Nearly 80 percent of new homes sold are financed with conventional thirty-year, fixed-interest-rate mortgage loans. Only about 5 percent of new homes are purchased with cash.

Translation: You're likely going to finance all or part of your new home. If you have owned or currently own a house and are paying down a loan for it, you know the drill of applying and gaining approval for a home mortgage. But financing a residential construction project, especially if you need to purchase land, has a much different set of rules depending on the condition of the parcel and what and when you plan to build on it.

If you're looking to buy land as opposed to building a house in a subdivision in which land is typically included in the price of the home, your best bet is either a cash deal or seller financing. That's because banks have little interest in loaning money to individuals for land purchases, especially for *raw* or *undeveloped* parcels that have no real or added value in the eyes of a *lender.*

Of course, the land itself is valuable; after all, there's a purchase price and you want it. But "real" value in lending lingo includes improvements such as utility lines to the property, curbs and gutters, and other *infrastructure,* and perhaps an existing

There are several ways to secure financing for land purchase, construction, and a home mortgage, though the rules and terms differ depending on the condition of the property and your plans to develop it.

building. Simply, banks are looking for assets on or to the property they can either sell or don't have to pay for to make it attractive to another buyer should you default on the loan.

Title: Legal documents indicating the right of ownership to real property.

Lenders are more willing to loan money for a raw land purchase, however, if you present a plan and a timeline for making improvements and building a home—the more specific the better, if possible including home plans for the parcel that have been approved for construction and/or a construction agreement with a contractor that outlines a production schedule. A spreadsheet of costs to bring utilities and pour a driveway to the site can also help tip the scales in your favor.

You can find land from several sources, occasionally from owners willing to help you finance the purchase, if necessary.

That effort can add up to quite an investment given that there's no guarantee you'll get the loan and ultimately purchase the land, so seek out lenders with a reputation or track record of land deals to find out their specific requirements for approving a loan.

In some cases, if you can't swing a cash purchase or a loan, the land seller may be willing and able to finance the deal. However, unlike a cash purchase or bank loan—after which you'll gain occupancy (if not the *title*) immediately—you likely won't be able to build (or get a construction loan) until you have paid in full and gained title to the property. No one wants to risk money for a home on a piece of land you don't yet own free and clear, not to mention the fact that you'll be carrying a debt that may preclude your ability to gain adequate construction financing.

Modern building systems, such as panelization, help speed the building process and convert higher-risk construction financing to permanent, long-term mortgage loans.

Once you're ready to build, you will have several options for financing the project. Of course, you may pay with cash, most likely in stages corresponding to the progress of your home's completion instead of a lump sum. Common sources of cash include a savings, checking, or penalty-free investment account (be careful not to delve into retirement and other tax-deferred funds unless you're willing to pay the price now *and* in the future). Cash can also come from an inheritance, lottery winnings, or, if you already own a home, perhaps a line of credit or loan based on your current home's equity.

The amount of a ***home equity*** loan, however, depends on how much you've paid down your mortgage principal (assuming you haven't ***refinanced*** recently) and/or whether your home has ***appreciated in value*** enough over the years to create a substantial difference between its ***assessed value*** now compared to when you secured its mortgage loan.

Home equity loans are made available in the form of either a lump sum, also called a second mortgage, or a line of credit, in which you are charged interest only on the amount drawn from a checking or debit account. They are usually ***secured loans*** used to partially or fully finance second homes, land purchases, construction, and/or outright ownership. For people financing a new primary residence, however, home equity loans often must be paid off before a bank or other lender will approve a mortgage loan for another house.

If you currently rent or have little equity in your current home, a separate construction loan is probably in order. More so than a mortgage loan, however, construction financing carries additional risks for the bank or lending institution because there is still no real, finished asset (that is, a completed house) adding value to the land.

As a consequence, a construction loan is likely to carry a higher interest rate and a smaller repayment window than a mortgage or equity loan—in fact, the balance will be due upon approved completion of the house, probably in less than a year's time. At that point most construction loans are converted to mortgage loans, also called permanent financing.

Construction-to-permanent (C2P) loans have become more popular as banks and their customers look to streamline paperwork, time, and *approvals* for funding residential projects. Essentially, the terms of your mortgage loan are agreed to when you gain access to construction money.

Banks like C2P loans because they maintain control of payments during construction and are assured of the mortgage loan when the house is completed and occupied; builders are warming up to C2Ps because they ensure more prompt payments from the bank and do not rely on the home buyer. Home buyers like the fact that the construction loan simply converts to a mortgage without additional time, hassle, or costs once the house is completed, and that they receive a certificate of occupancy (CO) and a modified tax assessment when the loan converts.

To cover their risk with a construction loan, even a C2P, banks are more finicky and often require a signed construction contract and *working drawings* of the house to be built. The lender may also want proof of approvals and *permits* for construction and *lien releases* from the builder as phases are finished and subcontractors are paid from the account.

Alternatives to conventional financing are also gaining momentum, as builders and suppliers of kit and manufactured homes seek more buyers. Because most of the country's largest home-building companies operate *in-house mortgage entities,* several smaller builders, lumberyards, and kit/manufactured home dealers either follow suit, offer their business lines of credit for funding, or work with an outside broker or bank to help home buyers gain access to funds.

Because of their manufacturing efficiencies, if on a different scale, both kit homes and manufactured homes are typically less expensive than the traditional, *stick-built home.* As a result, the amount of financing you need will likely be lower, allowing you to qualify for funds that come closer to affording your dreams.

Approvals: Consent by the appropriate building authority to issue a permit and begin construction once certain conditions (e.g., code-compliant building plans) are met.

Working drawings: The detailed plans or blueprints required for approvals or construction; also known as "construction drawings."

Permits: Documents proving acceptance and payment for various stages of construction to commence, which are posted at the home site and referred to by building inspectors to confirm proper construction methods and materials.

Lien releases: Documents that prove all claims for labor and materials costs have been paid in full or to the supplier's satisfaction; also known as "lien waiver."

In-house mortgage entities: Mortgage lending services provided or offered by the builder or supplier.

Stick-built home: A house built using only uncut or precut structural lumber.

To summarize, your financing options include:

- **Cash** (from savings, checking, or penalty-free investment accounts; inheritance), which can be used to purchase land or make necessary improvements and/or cover design costs to gain financing, if necessary.

- **Land seller financing,** which may preclude your ability to obtain construction financing.

- **Home equity loan or line of credit,** assuming you've owned your home for more than five years without refinancing or its value has appreciated enough to cover your financial needs.

- **Construction loan,** which is likely to carry a higher interest rate than a mortgage loan but may be necessary to finance part or all of the building process.

- **Construction-to-permanent (C2P) loan,** in which the construction loan amount and terms are converted to a mortgage loan on the finished home and property.

- **Supplier or builder financing,** also called in-house financing, in which the kit home supplier or home builder will finance the project and perhaps the mortgage loan to gain your business.

A Needs and Wants Assessment

Now that you have your financial house in order, it's time to see how far that money will go. There is no wrong answer here . . . and no universal formula. Even so, it's important to separate and prioritize needs from wants, just as you sorted essential and nonessential expenses to determine your affordability. Doing so enables you to set reliable expectations, avoid emotional and impulsive decisions, and objectively balance your dreams with reality.

There likely will be significant differences depending whether your new home is to be your primary residence or a second home. Each option opens a wide range of considerations regarding the home's location; proximity to schools, services, and recreational opportunities; applicable taxes, fees, and insurance risks; and even its size and style.

A needs and wants assessment is a matter of personal preference, but consider the following guidelines to get you started:

1. Take your time. Brainstorm some ideas early on, but keep the log open for ad hoc thoughts for at least a few weeks, if not until you're ready to start the design process.

2. Add graphics. Cut out photos from magazines and newspapers that spark ideas or show what you want or need.

3. Don't edit yourself . . . yet. Allow yourself to dream, knowing that eventually you'll probably have to scale back your ideas in the finished project.

4. Think ahead. This house will likely be one you'll want to live in for a while, so think about storage, the number of bedrooms and bathrooms, and family and entertainment space needs now and in the future.

5. Consider everything. A needs and wants assessment includes ideas about where you want to live (if not the actual building site), so think about issues of climate, proximity to services, *amenities,* schools, shopping, and where you work, as well as distances from other things (and people) in your life.

6. List what you don't want. Keep track of the things that bug you about your current house or homes you've seen or visited and vowed to eliminate or change if you ever had the chance. Now's your chance.

Amenities: Activities or features (such as walking paths, tennis courts, pool) to which residents of a community or the surrounding area have access.

NEEDS AND WANTS WORKSHEET

HOME	WANT	NEED	ACTIVITIES	WANT	NEED
Four bedrooms	☐	☑	Schools within walking/biking distance	☐	☑
Three full baths	☑	☐	YMCA	☑	☐
Big windows	☑	☐	Reading	☐	☑
Covered porch	☑	☐	Golf	☑	☐
Breakfast nook	☐	☑	Within 30 minutes' drive of work	☐	☑
Maple cabinets	☑	☐	Home theater	☑	☐
Berber carpet	☑	☐	Movie rental	☑	☐
Home office	☐	☑	Antiquing	☑	☐
Two-car garage w/shop	☐	☑	Vegetable garden	☐	☑
Small yard	☑	☐			

Once you have a big file compiled, start categorizing ideas into columns such as location/setting, interiors, exteriors, and whatever else seems appropriate (see the sample Needs and Wants Worksheet above; a blank version is at the back of the book). Then take an honest look at what's really needed and what you're willing to sacrifice for whatever reason. Create a separate list of items that you may be able to add over time, such as finishing a bonus room or attic. You may even eliminate items that you know are simply unrealistic or truly unnecessary, including a hot tub, outdoor kitchen, or pool.

An ideal needs and wants assessment starts out as a collection of ideas and photos and evolves into a clear-cut set of expectations and priorities, creating an ample reference for you or a design professional and contractor to create your new home. It is the backbone of your house plan and will, in large part, determine the type of construction method you eventually choose.

Finding and Developing Land

The setting in which you want to live—be it on the ocean or lakeside, in a small town, or in the suburbs—will largely come out of your needs and wants assessment. The actual parcel of land (also called the lot, **building pad,** or site) will be driven more by your budget and financing, schedule, and desired level of involvement.

Parcels of land, from single-home lots to small and large tracts for multiple homes, are available in every city and town.

Finding a piece of ground on which to build or place your house is infinitely easier once you know where you want to live. Even small towns have real estate agents and financial institutions that broker land deals; classified ads, real estate magazines, road signs, and the Internet are all viable options for finding what's available, learning the specifications and asking prices of those parcels, and beginning the negotiating process.

Essentially, you have three choices regarding a land purchase: raw land, developed land, or improved land.

Raw land is a parcel that is devoid of any services, existing structures, or other sign of improvement. It is unexcavated, nor is it clear of trees, shrubs, boulders, or other intrusions. Developed land is often cleared and may be *excavated* for a building pad, with basic utility services brought to the curb or the edge of the property line. Improved land is ready for construction, often with some features in place, such as a curb and gutter, utilities stubbed up to the location of the foundation or service main, and perhaps even a survey on file at the office of the reigning building authority.

In terms of cost, raw land is cheapest and improved land the most expensive, assuming a same or similar location: A raw piece of land along Lake Tahoe or in Myrtle Beach will likely be more expensive than an improved lot outside Omaha but less costly than a ready-to-build parcel elsewhere on the lake or coastline.

The three stages of land development, including raw land (top), developed parcels (middle, indicated by streets and curbs), and improved (bottom, with building pads and utilities in place). Raw land offers the most options for creating a lot for your new home, but it also requires the most work and cost to ready it for construction.

Regardless, a piece of raw land will need to be developed for the construction of a home, with all of the appropriate *soils tests,* engineering surveys, property borders, and service lines brought up to snuff.

The cost to turn raw land into a buildable parcel is expressed in time, money, and trade-offs, depending on the location. Before you buy a piece of raw land, have a clear understanding of available services such as water, electricity, natural gas, and telephone, and be prepared to make choices such as using a septic tank; solar, wood, or wind power; on-site propane; and cellular or satellite services—or go without—if you want to live in a rural or undeveloped area.

Rather than tackle the chore of developing a piece of raw land yourself, you may consider negotiating a certain level of improvements with the landowner as part of your purchase agreement; to what extent the seller is willing to do and charge, and what you're able to pay and/or wait for those improvements, is part of that negotiation.

In some cases, such as a resort development or a planned community or subdivision, the land is already improved and/or approved for a specific development plan. The catch, however, is that you typically must select from a short list of homes already approved to be built on those lots, or adhere to strict *design criteria* and *review mechanisms,* instead of being in full control of your home's layout, size, style, and finishes.

Remember, too, that land in any state of readiness or improvement carries property taxes and should be insured. Those two costs will undoubtedly go up once your house is finished and the overall value of the property is reassessed . . . expenses most likely included in your monthly mortgage payment, especially on a primary residence.

As daunting as they may seem on their own, however, land costs represent only a fraction of the overall expenses you can anticipate for your new home project.

Calculating Costs

In addition to land and any necessary improvements to it, the costs to create a new home fall into three basic categories: design, construction, and maintenance. Each category offers not only a wide range of choices but also a matrix of smaller costs that are either ongoing or up front (see the Ongoing and Up-front Costs Worksheet at the back of the book).

Construction costs, for instance, include materials, labor, equipment, excavation, management, waste removal, and perhaps temporary power and shipping, among other direct and indirect expenses. These are considered up-front costs because they will be spent only during a finite amount of time instead of over the life of the house.

Oh, and there's another cost category . . . one that's the most difficult to calculate but that must be considered: your time. Suffice it to say at this point that your time, based on the role you decide to play in the process, should not be discounted or neglected in your cost calculations. While it may not be expressed in actual dollars you pay yourself, your time away from work, family, and other fun activities to focus on your housing project has a cost. If you really want to see its dollar impact, calculate your time as an hourly rate (perhaps based on your salary); estimate how much time you're willing or able to devote to the project on a daily, weekly, and/or monthly basis; and add it up. Even then you won't be able to assess the real impact of spending time and energy away from others and other activities.

Unlike ongoing costs, such as a utility bill, up-front costs are rarely charged consistently. Despite that dynamic, consider trying to level (or at least translate) those expenses to a reliable amount per month. Doing so will not only help match costs to your affordability (the calculation done earlier) but also avoid a roller coaster of account balances or, worse, put a halt to a project in progress until a lump-sum payment is made.

Construction expenses, including materials shipping, are calculated as up-front costs, as they will occur only during the building process, prior to occupancy.

Elevations: Two-dimensional renderings or representations of a vertical surface (such as a wall).

Options: Alternatives to what is standard or offered in the basic house at no additional charge.

For instance, the price of land and design fees can perhaps be spread out over time, albeit in terms of months instead of years, to avoid lump-sum payments. The distribution of construction funds, also a relatively short-term agreement, is usually based on percentage of verified completion, sometimes by the lender and/or building inspector, but also (or perhaps only) by the home buyer. Don't settle for lump-sum payments at any phase of the project—especially during construction—unless you can either afford it or it's absolutely necessary or contractually obligated.

Design Costs

The design of your new home will come with a cost, but maybe nothing out of pocket. Homes from a catalog or a factory take the design process—and fees—away from outside architects and other professionals by providing a growing number of house plans, *elevations,* and *options,* as well as working drawings and details necessary to construct the home.

A difficult but necessary cost to calculate is your time—especially if you plan to be a hands-on home owner during the construction phase.

Because they are already designed and engineered, house plans from a kit home catalog or manufactured home builder are less expensive than original or even modified plans from an architect or traditional home builder. An architect may charge 20 percent of the overall project costs to develop and design a complete set of drawings for your project; a plan from a kit home catalog or manufactured home builder is perhaps a tenth of that. If at all. With few exceptions, design costs for kit homes are included in the cost of the materials package (or kit). The only time you might pay for a set of kit home plans is if you decide not to purchase materials and "shop" the drawings to other suppliers or a lumberyard for a better price . . . and even then, the plans will likely only cost a few hundred dollars. The price of a manufactured home always includes the design; given engineering and machinery differences, the house plans of one company cannot be built by another.

Design costs may come into play for kit homes when the buyer asks for custom changes to the plan or elevations—changes that are not part of the manufacturing process and therefore reduce the efficiency of the building system, adding costs. In such cases, the kit home company or lumberyard may have an in-house designer, draftsperson, or sales associate capable of making the changes (likely on a computer in front of the buyer) and assessing the extra expense.

Or the home buyer may take the plans to an outside design professional, most likely a draftsperson rather than an architect, to make the changes—for a separate fee. From there the kit home supplier will reestimate the price to supply the materials package from which to build the home based on the changes made.

Building Costs

As mentioned, construction costs run the gamut from mobilization (getting the crew ready and equipped to start building) to the painters and carpet installers just before *move-in.*

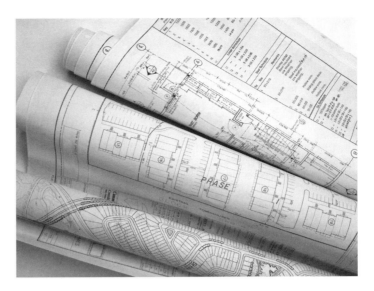

For kit homes, the costs are similar to a stick-built home because that's essentially what you're doing . . . with a predesigned plan and precut, engineered framing components instead of traditional lumber. Kit homes from a catalog require a foundation and other hardscapes (like a driveway or patio); rough and finish electrical, plumbing, and heating/cooling systems; insulation and *drywall;* windows and doors; and exterior and interior finishes. You may want a garage, which may be part of the kit but still needs a *slab foundation* and assembly on-site.

Kit homes also require the cost of the contractor and subcontractors (or specialty trades, such as a plumber), unless you tackle the job of the general contractor and perhaps some of the specialty trades yourself. Even if you do, there are costs involved—perhaps not direct monetary costs, but certainly in terms of your time away from work, your family, and other activities. It's up to you to calculate the cost of stress as well.

Without knowing your specific circumstances, wants, and needs, it's impossible to say how much a kit home will cost or what you'll need to spend beyond the building package offered by the kit home manufacturer or lumberyard. That number depends not only on the size and complexity of the house but also on the extent of the package provided and the contractors involved. The best advice is to make sure you consider and refine all of the aspects of your project and compare costs fairly and equitably to determine your costs.

Chapter 3 includes a detailed discussion of building cost efficiencies for kit homes, such as engineered roof trusses and other factory-built framing components.

Manufactured homes, by contrast, take much of the on-site construction costs away by building 90 percent of the home in a factory. Upon delivery to your lot, manu-

Securing a full set of construction drawings is another up-front cost to calculate, though some kit (and all HUD-code) home suppliers credit or factor that cost into their materials pricing or finished home cost.

Move-in: Occupancy.

Drywall: Sheets (or panels) of gypsum-based wallboard used instead of plaster to cover interior wall and ceiling framing members; also known as Sheetrock, a brand name of United States Gypsum.

Slab foundation: An at-grade, monolithic section of concrete that serves as the structural base of the house or other building.

factured homes are fully plumbed, insulated, drywalled, and finished with trim, carpet or other flooring, appliances, light fixtures, outlets and switches, and roofing and siding. It's a one-stop shopping experience . . . almost.

All a manufactured home needs, in fact, is a *pad* or foundation, utility hook-ups, and a few trim pieces to hide the interior and exterior seams where two or more sections are joined to create the finished home. These days manufactured home owners, whether on rural lots or in subdivisions designed for such buildings (*very* different from trailer parks), also opt to build stick-framed or kit garages for their homes. With a detached or attached garage, modern manufactured homes are almost indistinguishable from one-story site-built homes.

That bit of extra, site-built construction will likely require the cost and time of a contractor or two, but far less than a kit or stick-built home. In fact, many local manufactured home dealers are also called builders because they offer or provide the skills and/or crews to perform these tasks. At the very least, they are contractually obligated to deliver and *set* the home on its foundation and make it ready for occupancy.

As a result of building the vast majority of the home off-site, manufactured homes not only cost less than a comparably sized and finished site-built home but also are completed faster. Reducing what builders call "cycle time"—the amount of time between the start of construction and a home's completion—is a tremendous cost savings. Time, after all, is money.

There is one atypical cost associated with manufactured housing, however: shipping. It's a cost that must be considered and calculated; the farther you are from the factory, the more it will cost to ship the home to your site. By contrast, the cost to deliver building materials to your home site from a local lumberyard is often waived or at least built into the costs of the lumber and other components being shipped.

Some of the biggest manufactured and *modular* home builders have multiple factory locations across the country, but only a few will ship farther than 200 to 300 miles away from those locations. Chances are good, however, that you will find an acceptable manufactured home builder or dealer serving the area in which you want to live.

Whether you choose a kit home from a catalog or a manufactured home, the discussion of price will occur early on. Home packages and certainly manufactured homes—and their available options and *upgrades*—are *prepriced* and easy to calculate and evaluate.

The good news is that even if a kit home package does not include everything you want (few do), the supplier will have estimates and contacts to help you fill in the blanks and calculate the total cost. Manufactured homes, as mentioned, are nearly a one-stop shopping experience, including pricing. Dealers are able and willing to help estimate the cost and time to get the house and site ready and completed.

Maintenance Costs

For the most part, this cost is up to you. Your lifestyle, the size of the house you built or purchased, and your local utility and other service costs will determine ongoing expenses.

Specific to energy costs, modern manufactured homes are especially efficient, given the factory-controlled environment in which they are built and the federal building codes and standards required for their construction.

Kit homes can be built just as efficiently and according to building codes and federal energy-efficient home program guidelines and products, but the quality is inherently less consistent than factory-built homes. Simply, you're relying on less-controlled labor and materials quality. Also, while a site-built home may be inspected a half-dozen times during construction to make sure it complies with the local building code, a manufactured home is inspected perhaps a dozen or more times in the factory.

For a kit home, work with your builder and/or supplier to set expectations for the home's overall performance and maintenance. You may select, for instance, a higher grade of windows or insulation, roofing and siding materials, or heating and cooling equipment—all for an upgraded cost, of course, but balanced against lower upkeep and utility bills.

Other ongoing, operating, or maintenance costs include property taxes, homeowner's insurance (a smart investment even if you don't have a mortgage; required if you do have a mortgage), homeowner association fees that pay for the maintenance of common space and amenities as well as general oversight of the development or neighborhood, and nonessential utilities or services. If you're building a second home, factor in expenses for transportation, caretaking, furniture, food, and the use of nearby recreational facilities or amenities. If your budget maximum looms, decide what you need and want to have now as opposed to items or expenses that can be added over time.

Inspections: Periodically scheduled mandatory checks conducted by a third party to ensure a house is being built according to the approved plans and specifications.

Walk-throughs: Tours of a house under construction or recently completed.

Change orders: Requests by the home owner to alter the agreed plans or specifications.

Determining Your Role

There are plenty of books out there trumpeting the virtues of acting as your own contractor. For a kit home and the relatively small amount of work required to prepare or supplement a manufactured home, that option is certainly available. So is simply signing a few contracts with professional tradespeople and waiting for the phone to ring with a move-in date.

The most important role you'll play in the project, however, is that of the home buyer. Never forget that this is *your* house and that you are entitled to ask questions, make decisions, gain assurances, and be completely satisfied.

It's also your role to investigate your options thoroughly in terms of the type of construction method (kit or manufactured) that's best for your circumstances. It's on you to select a builder and/or subcontractors you can work with and who will respect your comfort level, and to guide the overall process as the home buyer.

It's a responsibility that requires you to be reasonably educated about the building process and to set realistic expectations and standards with yourself and your kit or manufactured home supplier and building team. Establish an agreed method of communication and meeting expectations, and you've set the stage for managing the majority of the issues you'll confront.

In addition, there will be deadlines to meet for decisions such as adding upgrades and options, making floor plan changes, and choosing interior and exterior finishes; there will (or should) be procedures for *inspections, walk-throughs,* and *change orders.*

These deadlines and procedures are rarely arbitrary. In fact, they are part of what makes kit and manufactured homes efficient and lower-cost building alternatives to traditional site-built homes.

As the home buyer, the *best thing you can do* is to understand and respect the process, meet deadlines, and follow agreed procedures and processes for communication during the project.

By taking responsibility for your role and following through at every opportunity, you'll set an example for the entire project team to follow, whether you're swinging a hammer or not.

Ready to Build?

Not yet. There's a little matter of selecting the home building process—a kit home or a manufactured home—before you break ground. But if you've prepared for that decision properly and thoroughly, as outlined on the previous pages, you've created a solid platform from which to make that decision.

"We've always envisioned our home as the perfect retreat. While collaborating with Classic, we saw our vision come to life. It was a five-star experience."
– Jack Curran

IT ALL BEGINS WITH YOU...

Riverbend
TIMBER FRAMING
Established 1979

the historic homes of the future.

Featuring "Easy-Panel Wall System"

Homes from a Catalog

IMAGINE BEING ABLE TO SELECT a home from a catalog, make a few changes to accommodate your location and lifestyle, receive a full set of *construction drawings* and instructions for a fraction of the cost of an architect, and order the delivery of all the materials you'll need to build and finish the house of your dreams.

What was true nearly a century ago through the mail-order wizardry of Sears, Roebuck & Company's Modern Homes program has been expanded and refined today through a matrix of printed and online house plan resources, kit home suppliers, and local lumberyards.

But while Sears and its handful of contemporaries in the first half of the twentieth century each offered a choice of a few hundred homes (and several of the same model with simply a different exterior finish), today's house plan sources publish tens of thousands of home designs, with the ability to alter any floor plan, elevation, and other details to accommodate your lifestyle needs, your budget, and your aesthetic tastes.

True, the cost of today's house plans can't match the one-dollar price tag Sears put on a complete set of blueprints (a cost that was then credited toward the purchase of the building materials package for that house, also through Sears), but they're still a remarkably affordable design option. The price of a complete set of construction drawings for a 2,705-square-foot, two-story Craftsman-style home found through an online plan source, including some extra paperwork and alterations, is quoted at $1,815 (US). That's less than 5 percent of what a typical architect might charge to design a comparable house.

Construction of a house plan purchased from a printed or online catalog also can be more cost efficient than traditional building methods, especially if you select a materials package or kit home with the pieces and parts already cut to size or fabricated in a factory and ready to assemble on your home site. Quality control of the materials and their assembly in a factory, and stricter adherence to building codes among kit home suppliers, arguably delivers a higher level of durability.

Sears and other mail-order home suppliers pioneered the precut home package concept, as well as stock home plan alterations, steel framing, *in-house financing,* inte-

---

Be sure to use the extensive catalogs of house plan publishers and kit home package suppliers provided at the end of this chapter, including some helpful hints about using the catalog to narrow your choices.

Construction drawings:
The detailed plans or blueprints used by the builder and various contractors during construction; also known as "working drawings."

In-house financing:
Lending services or loans offered by the builder; also known as "private financing."

Plated roof trusses are now standard in modern home construction.

Semicustom: A basic house plan or house features altered to accommodate lifestyle or other needs without sacrificing production efficiencies.

Bid estimates, bids: Estimated costs for construction provided by builders or contractors.

Timber frame: A type of construction using heavy-duty structural timbers in a post-and-beam configuration.

Log home: A kit or stick-built house constructed of (or to replicate) logs from cut trees.

Prefab housing, a derivative of modular and panelized construction, often delivers contemporary home styles.

rior finish packages, and a selection of like-styled homes offered to developers that are seen today. As it was then, these and other innovations are offered now as an affordable, high-quality, easy-to-build, *semicustom* housing option.

These days there are essentially two ways to purchase a home from a catalog, each of which is explained in detail in this chapter.

The first is to buy a set of construction drawings, or blueprints, through a house plan publisher or online service (such as the example mentioned earlier). The plans are then used to hire a builder (or so you can be your own builder), gather *bid estimates* from trade contractors, procure the materials from local suppliers, and construct the home.

The second is to work with a prefab housing, home package, or kit home company, from which you select a house plan from a proprietary catalog and receive a complete materials package shipped to your home site for you and/or a builder and various trade contractors to assemble and finish. Kit home suppliers range from those that specialize in *timber frame* and *log home* styles to local lumberyards providing a variety of traditional and regionally appropriate housing styles to prefab companies offering contemporary forms.

There's a lot of variation and crossover within those two basic methods, such as a lumberyard that leverages a house plan publisher's catalog to sell home packages, or a log home company that provides a list of builders in your area who are familiar with the company's sales and delivery processes, construction drawings, and/or building system to grease the wheels of a sale.

The range of home styles available from either source is nearly endless when you consider the ability to alter the floor plan, elevations, details, and even the foundation and framing system to suit your home site, local building codes, lifestyle, surrounding neighborhood, budget, or personal taste—while still remaining affordable.

Of course, the more changes you make to a house plan or kit home—or are required to make to suit a difficult terrain (such as a hillside or an oceanfront lot) or meet local building code requirements—the more costs you incur. The chances of outpacing an architect's budget to create original house plans, however, are still remote.

You can avoid feeling overwhelmed by the possibilities and number of decisions you need to make, even at the design stage, by spending the time to specifically assess and prioritize your needs, wants, finances, and role as the home owner (see chapter 2). Armed with that knowledge and discipline, the process of buying and building a home from a catalog can be an enjoyable, time-saving, and economical adventure.

The Design Process

Regardless of which of the two primary methods you choose to purchase a home from a catalog, the process for determining the style, size, floor plan, and finishes of your home is similar. Each, however, has its quirks, and it's critical to be aware of their respective nuances before you make a purchasing decision.

House Plans from a Catalog Publisher

Until and since the advent of the Internet and World Wide Web, house plans (also called *stock home plans*) have been published in catalogs containing hundreds of different housing styles and configurations. Each plan is typically shown with an illustrated rendering of what the home looks like from the street (or front elevation) and floor plan (for as many floors as there are) and provides a brief marketing description. You also get the measurement of the home's overall square footage, footage by floor (including the basement and garage, if applicable), and its width and depth in feet. In some cases the rendering may be in three dimensions to provide an extra measure of perspective.

Such catalogs, also referred to as *house plan books,* are available in grocery and drugstore magazine racks, retail and online bookstores, and the library. Many house

Stock home plans:
Predesigned house plans.

House plan books:
Printed catalogs of stock home plans.

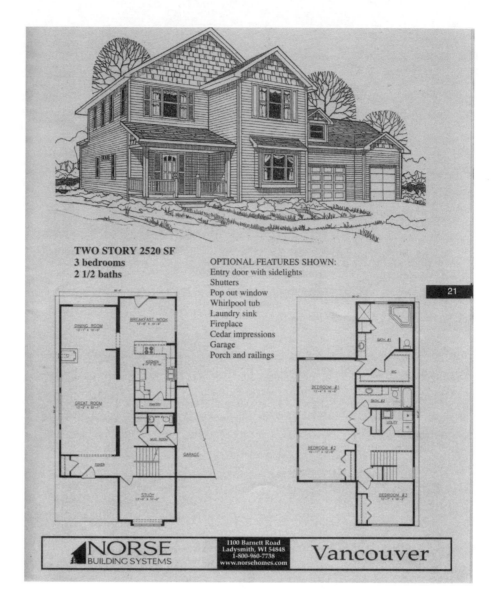

TWO STORY 2520 SF
3 bedrooms
2 1/2 baths

OPTIONAL FEATURES SHOWN:
Entry door with sidelights
Shutters
Pop out window
Whirlpool tub
Laundry sink
Fireplace
Cedar impressions
Garage
Porch and railings

NORSE BUILDING SYSTEMS

1100 Barnett Road
Ladysmith, WI 54848
1-800-960-7738
www.norsehomes.com

Vancouver

plan book publishers offer Internet Web sites, where buyers can search for, select, request changes to, and receive pricing and other ordering details online. Internet buyers are considered "unescorted" in stock plan lingo, as opposed to those who phone or mail in their order and are shepherded (or "escorted") through the process by a customer service or sales representative. Online sales for one of the largest home plan publishers currently accounts for about 40 percent of the company's sales.

Many more stock plan sources, including individual architects and home designers, sell their designs exclusively online, banking on the increasing use of and familiarity with the Internet among consumers while saving the expense of printing and distributing catalogs and managing call-in orders. A keyword search for "home plans" on a popular online search engine revealed more than 8.7 million possible links.

Print and virtual (Internet) publishers also offer specialty stock plan catalogs by certain types or styles of homes, such as Craftsman, traditional, waterfront, and vacation houses, among several other categories, to help house plan shoppers narrow their choices to a few hundred from among a total library of perhaps 10,000 stock plans available from a single publisher. Some sources offer deck and porch plans and landscape design blueprints that can be adapted for several housing styles.

The plans found in these books and on their Web counterparts are owned wholly or in part by the publishers. These companies either develop original plans using in-house design teams, purchase full ownership rights from design professionals, or negotiate their availability and sale with outside architects and designers.

In fact, some of the country's best-known and prolific residential architects and design professionals are contracted by home plan publishers to sell a selection of their original and most-popular work.

Occasionally a contract with an outside designer limits the availability of **study (or review) sets,** allowable changes, or **multiple-use rights** by a home owner, which may sway your decision to purchase the plan for your project. In most cases, however, the home plan publisher has the right to sell the plans as it would those it has developed in-house.

House plan books may contain helpful articles about selecting a plan, finding a contractor, and the plan-ordering process. Of course, they provide detailed instructions for ordering a study set of the plan or a complete, construction-ready set of blueprints and other items included in that package.

Both online and printed order forms allow you to request changes, for a price premium, including a different type of foundation or garage configuration (see the "Making Changes" section, page 45). You can purchase additional documentation and detail drawings to help gather bid estimates from contractors and/or materials suppliers, such as a local lumberyard.

The only real advantage to using an online house plan catalog is the speed at which you can narrow your choices among the stock plans available from that publisher or supplier. Changes or alterations for each plan are provided as a reference to help further refine your search, but changes cannot be made online; instead, you must submit and

Study (or review) sets:
Less-detailed sets of blueprints provided to a potential plan or home buyer for review purposes.

Multiple-use rights:
Authorization or restrictions regarding the use of a stock home plan more than one time.

Home plan publishers offer value-added services, such as informational articles and plans for landscaping and ancillary features, as well as convenient online access.

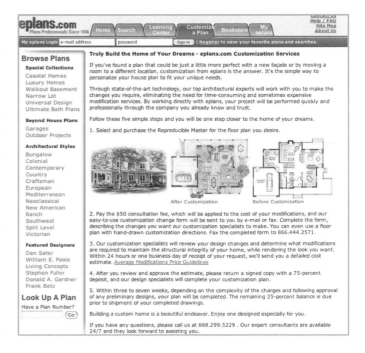

Raised-floor framing:
A type of construction in which the first floor is built over a basement or crawl space.

Mechanical runs:
The length of the wires, cables, ductwork, and plumbing pipes from their respective sources (e.g., the furnace) to various rooms in the house.

pay for them as part of your order, just as you would through the mail using a printed catalog.

Generally, the basic set of construction drawings you'll receive includes a cover (or frontal) page that shows a rendering of the home's front elevation, provides general notes, and defines the abbreviations and architectural symbols on the set of plans enclosed (see the "Common Symbols" sidebar below). A subsequent page shows renderings of the home's back and side elevations as well as an aerial view of the roof to indicate its design.

In addition, the basic set provides a foundation plan with pertinent structural information (such as a *raised-floor framing* layout) and the layout and location of heating, ventilating, and air-conditioning (HVAC) ductwork and other *mechanical runs.* Other pages show the structural framing plan and details for each floor of the house, as well as selected interior elevations, such as the kitchen and bathrooms, to help estimate cabinet, countertop, major plumbing, and appliance purchases.

Finally, home plan suppliers provide electrical layouts and locations for each level of the house (including a basement foundation and section details for stairs and fireplaces, among other areas) to help direct their construction.

Common Symbols

Construction documents include a language all their own to identify areas, features, or instructions in a limited amount of space on the blueprints. Here are a few symbols and abbreviations you'll likely see on a set of plans:

KS: Knee space
WIC: Walk-in closet
FPL: Fireplace
O/C: On-center spacing (which defines the spacing between studs, joists, rafters, or other structural framing members)
SIM: Similar
TYP: Typical
AC: Air conditioner/air-conditioning
ADD: Addendum or addition
BSMT: Basement
BG: Below ground/grade
CND: Conduit
CSK: Countersink (pushing the head of a fastener below the surface of the material)

1/C or 2/C: Single or double conductor (through which heat, electricity, or water is transferred)
DS: Downspout
DHW: Double-hung window
EW: Each way (indicating the dual direction of a pipe or wire)
FLG: Flooring
FOC: Free of charge
NS: Not specified
REM: Removable
SOV: Shutoff valve
S4S: Surfaced on four sides (a component that is ready to finish or already finished on all four sides)
WC: Water closet (toilet)

A home plan service will typically offer or suggest the purchase of multiple sets of complete blueprints (usually four or five) for use in gathering bid estimates from contractors and materials suppliers as well as to distribute to your chosen contractors once work begins on your house. Each extra set carries an additional cost of about $50 each (depending on the seller) but is a necessary expense, as some plan publishers prohibit you from making more copies once you receive the plans. Publishers may offer packaged sets (four or eight sets each, for instance) at a more economical price per print than buying them individually or in odd lots.

Vellum: A house plan or construction document in reproducible format.

An alternative to buying multiple sets is to purchase a set of *vellum,* or reproducible, prints. A vellum set allows you to make as many copies as you need, when you need them, without losing the resolution (or detail) of the original plan. Vellum plans, however, carry a higher initial cost than a nonreproducible set of blueprints.

Even if you buy a vellum set of plans, the plan source may limit their use for the construction of only one house. A one-time or limited-use rights clause in your purchasing agreement with a home plan publisher protects the value of the plans from you or a builder purchasing a single set and profiting from the sale of multiple homes derived from that one set of plans. Plans by an outside architect or designer, available through a stock plan publisher or independently sold, are more likely protected by single-use rights.

House plan publishers vary in their rules regarding use rights, however, with some acknowledging or even encouraging buyers (primarily those who are professional builders and developers) to use them over and over again. Following in the footsteps of Sears and other mail-order home suppliers, a few modern home plan companies entice their contractor customers to purchase sets of plans of like-styled homes to use in the development of a new housing tract or neighborhood. One source, in fact, has branded its approach "Neighborhood in a Box."

For most home owners, even owner-builders, the chances of building more than one home from a set of stock house plans is remote; few have the need, much less the gumption or financial means, to build more than one version of their dream home.

Beyond the Basic Set

The more sophisticated stock plan publishers also offer extra documentation to help prepare and guide you through the building process—for an additional, if nominal, charge.

A materials checklist is often a helpful addition to make sure you are aware of all that's needed to build and finish your home and as a way to keep your budget in check (or help determine your construction budget). Other documents may include

Specifications: The written requirements for materials, equipment, construction systems, and standards.

Model building codes: Standards approved for adoption and enforcement by state or local building departments or authorities.

Turnkey: Start to finish, completely.

Customization: Altering a stock house plan to suit lifestyle or other needs.

cost estimates for construction based on local market averages (derived from your city and zip code) as well as a specification outline that tracks the building process.

Detail sets, meanwhile, provide generic electrical, plumbing, mechanical, and construction *specifications* that comply with *model building codes* (but will still require local review), as well as methods and advice to assist owner-builders regardless of the plan selected.

House Plans from a Kit Home Provider

The process for selecting a house design from the catalog of a kit home, home package, or prefab provider is similar to choosing a stock house plan. The difference is that a kit home provider will offer plans only for the kits or packages it sells, but it supplies the basic (or sometimes complete) materials package for those plans, similar to the way Sears and others served the housing market a century ago. Many kit home companies also lobby to be your builder to create a *turnkey* or one-stop shopping experience for your housing needs.

With regards to the design process, the result of this scenario is a far smaller selection of basic plans, from a few dozen to perhaps a few hundred that are within the standard engineering and manufacturing limitations and materials inventory of the kit home company or lumberyard.

That said, these companies recognize the realities of today's home-buying market regarding *customization,* and they have figured out how to maintain their relative affordability compared to traditional building methods while allowing changes to their stock plans and manufacturing processes (see the "Making Changes" section that follows). Yes, those changes come at a cost, as they do when altering stock house plans, but the prices of the majority of alterations are predetermined to help maintain the economy of the home package or kit concept.

In addition to their ability to make slight changes to the plans they offer themselves, some kit suppliers and lumberyards can simply create or take a set of someone else's construction drawings and materials list (as you might purchase from a home plans publisher or catalog) and fill the order as they would for any building project.

In fact, many kit home and home package companies have designers on staff to help select, alter, or create a plan to suit your needs and circumstances; some allow you to hire an architect to design a custom home to the specifications of the kit supplier's building system. A lumberyard may offer a few dozen preengineered and prepriced home packages, thousands of stock home plans for which it will supply materials, and the option to create a custom plan with its in-house designers.

Online plan catalogs from a seemingly endless number of publishers, including independent architects and designers, provide you with an incredible amount of choice at your convenience. Unlike printed plan catalogs, the online versions are free.

Choosing a home from a kit company or lumberyard's library, however, is the best way to leverage the time and cost efficiencies of the home package concept. The plans have already been engineered (and perhaps code approved for the local market), and most of the high-volume and "generic" materials (such as insulation, drywall, and windows) are in stock, creating an economy of scale.

In addition, the supplier or lumberyard's manufacturing systems are geared to create a complete materials package per the prints in the company's catalog, saving time and labor. For these and other reasons, the vast majority of kit home and home package sales are from in-house design catalogs.

Though many kit home and home package suppliers market themselves online or with interactive CD-ROMs or DVDs, occasionally featuring three-dimensional video tours through some of their homes to provide even more perspective on design, few enable you to actually purchase a house package "unescorted" through the design process. You will be required at least to work with a sales associate over the phone or perhaps visit a nearby satellite office or design center to select and finalize the plan.

Like stock house plans, the design you choose from a kit home supplier or local lumberyard or home center—altered or not—is used to create the materials package needed to build the house. In this case, the same company that offers the plan also supplies the materials.

That package—typically including all necessary structural frame components, insulation and drywall, and exterior siding, roofing, and decorative trim—is delivered to your home site unassembled (see the "Building Options" section, beginning on page 54). Extra sets of plans and building instructions, among other documentation, accompany the package for you or your builder and trade contractors to estimate their labor costs and to refer to during construction.

During the design phase several kit home companies, and especially lumberyards, offer interior finish packages that supplement the basic materials set. Many set up in-house design centers and professional design consultants to help you select paints and stains, countertops, cabinets, flooring, interior trim, and perhaps appliances and furniture as part of your house package order. Otherwise, it's your responsibility to budget for, find, buy, and install those products to complete your home.

Modern showrooms are stocked with samples of the latest finishes for cabinets, flooring, lighting, plumbing fixtures, and windows and doors, among others. Showrooms allow you and your builder to browse and make selections for your finished home, and they provide a more tangible experience than choosing products from a printed or online catalog.

Unlike stock home plan publishers, a kit home company typically uses the design process to sell the materials package—similar to the way Sears and others did by charging just a dollar for a complete set of plans. As a result the design costs, including alterations, may be absorbed (or credited) in the cost of the materials package and/or the construction fee if you also hire the company to build your house.

However, if you choose a plan but decide not to purchase the materials from the company and instead shop them to other materials suppliers (such as another lumberyard or kit home provider), expect to be charged a fee for the design work, construction drawings, and copyrights as you would from a stock plan publisher. Even then you'll likely have to make (and pay for) additional changes to the plans to comply with the nuances of another materials supplier.

Making Changes

Home plan publishers and kit home suppliers are increasingly willing and able to accommodate a wide variety of changes to their plans, the latter to the point of allowing a custom design from a source other than their own catalogs.

Realizing that consumers are looking for the ability to customize stock plans for lifestyle and other reasons, these companies possess both the staff and the technology to manage plan alterations. They also realize that while stock plans, sans changes, are cost and time efficient, allowing changes is a lucrative profit center or an effective way to secure the sale of a materials package or kit.

To marry the two masters of economy and customization, stock plan sources and kit home suppliers develop customization or plan alteration lists, with a corresponding price range or estimate for each item. On one stock plan publisher's list, for instance, the price for adding or removing a garage from the blueprints is between $480 and $800 above the cost of the basic set, while switching from a crawl-space design to a full-basement plan might add $200 or more to the price of the plans.

Other alterations, such as enlarging a room or making the house wheelchair accessible, require price quotes based on a *per-square-foot basis.* Many companies offer checklists of allowable changes that you fill out and submit for a price quote, either online, in the mail, or over the phone, to create the design and construction drawings you want.

Other options are available. For instance, if you find a plan you like but simply want a mirror image of it, called a *reverse plan,* most stock plan publishers will accommodate that request for a small fee—and a higher premium if you want the words and symbols to read correctly instead of backward.

Per-square-foot basis:
A method for calculating costs based on a square foot of area; also known as "square-foot basis."

Reverse plan:
A mirror image of a house plan.

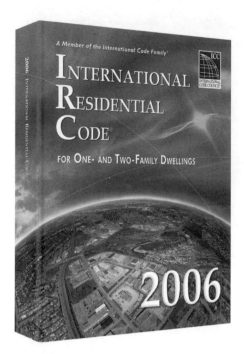

Code Compliance

Even though stock house plans are produced in compliance with national or one of the regional building code standards, most publishers and sellers suggest that you submit the plans for local building code approval to ensure compliance and to obtain building permits for construction, if required. Simply, your town, county, or state may enforce a slightly different interpretation of a given building code, and your plans (and the eventual house) will need to meet them before you are granted permits and certificate of occupancy, or CO. Only slight alterations, if any, are likely necessary to meet code, but they may require the services of an outside architect, engineer, contractor, or other design or building professional skilled in making the necessary changes and working with the local building department to get your plans approved and permitted.

The International Residential Code *is the industry guide to health and safety, among other regulations, governing all one- and two-family homes except manufactured homes, which are regulated by the HUD code.*

Legally, any changes made to a plan—either by the source or your own, local design professional or draftsperson—are considered to be "derivative works." As such, they remain protected by copyright laws subject to the same use rights as the original version, including rules about making unauthorized copies.

The advantage of using a stock plan publisher's or kit home supplier's in-house design team to make alterations is that you are assured that the changes are made to your satisfaction and remain "buildable." Lumberyards that sell home packages from stock plan catalogs often are contractually obligated to direct changes to those plans through the catalog company, but they will accommodate changes to plans in their own portfolios using in-house or local designers.

The bottom line is that almost all stock plan publishers and kit home suppliers allow you to make myriad changes to their plans. How companies manage alterations, and what and how they charge for them, varies as widely as the possible changes themselves.

Selecting a Contractor

As mentioned in chapter 2, acting as your own general contractor or builder is certainly an option for those who have the time, skills, and interest to manage a job site. For the vast majority of home buyers, especially those facing the prospect of ordering and assembling a kit of building materials dropped on their eventual doorstep into a finished house, hiring professionals is likely to be the preferred option.

From the self-help resources created for consumers to hire contractors, it's common advice to gather at least three **bids** and choose the lowest one. This is commonly called the "three-bid rule." The theory assumes that all three contractors are equally reputable and experienced in comparable projects (building an entire house) *and* have evaluated and estimated the project similarly. Those are some pretty big—and notoriously false—assumptions that often result in costly mistakes.

While it is possible with diligent effort to find, research, and properly prepare three reputable contractors to deliver comparable bid estimates for your project, it is equally possible (and more rewarding and assuring) to find one builder who has the skills, relevant experience, management capability, and compatible personality to work with you to build your home within your predetermined budget. This "negotiated contract" approach replaces the three-bid rule, with less risk of mistakes and poor estimating and a better chance for overall success and satisfaction with the building process.

The work you did to prepare for the project in chapter 2 is the foundation for selecting a general contractor and the various trade contractors (such as plumbers and electricians) needed to complete your home. With a budget and financing in hand, wants and needs established, and your role in the project determined, you have the basics for not only finding a house plan or kit home, but for hiring a team of contractors to help make it a reality.

Finding a Contractor

A few stock plan publishers provide a list of contractors in your area who have, at some level, qualified themselves as reputable and experienced builders. It may be that they are simply customers of the plan provider and are thus familiar with the company's procedures and level of detail regarding its construction documents and know how to alter them to meet local building codes and specific site and soil conditions.

Kit home manufacturers, especially log and timber-frame home suppliers, often have a network of qualified and experienced builders who are familiar—or perhaps even company certified—with their building systems. These builders may work exclusively for the kit home company, providing it with local marketing, sales, plan selection, and design coordination services, in addition to being builders of the company's products.

Similarly, lumberyards that sell home packages may offer to build at least the structural frame and perhaps the entire exterior envelope as part of the plan and materials package sale, referred to in the industry as *installed sales.*

Bids, bid estimates: Estimated costs for construction provided by builders or contractors.

Installed sales: When a supplier (e.g., lumberyard or home center) agrees or offers to install a product as a condition of the sale of that product.

In either case, you are (or should be) under no obligation to hire the kit home's local builder or the lumberyard's framing crew to build the home packages they supply. While the majority of kit home buyers choose the company's recommended local contractor (as he or she is often the buyer's primary or only contact with the supplier during the design process *and* is intimately familiar with the kit supplier's building system), kit home companies are willing to work with your selected builder without penalty. Lumberyards have no qualms working with a local builder, either, as it is an opportunity to serve an existing contractor customer or gain a new one through the experience.

Replacing the yellow pages and other sources, online directories—from both national and local sources—enable you to quickly and conveniently find those builders and contractors in your area.

Construction manager: The person in charge of the job site during construction; also known as "site superintendent," "lead," or "CM."

Contractor lists provided by home plan publishers and kit home companies are a good place to start but are by no means the only source. A fair number of the builders listed on the plan publisher's Web site may prefer to sell you a home they've already built or plan to build or to build you a home in a neighborhood they're developing rather than construct a custom home on your lot. A kit home builder may simply be a bad personality fit or a better salesperson than a *construction manager.*

Supplement such lists or create your own by asking friends, coworkers, and acquaintances for references. Check the local yellow pages and home builder's trade association chapter for custom builders and general contractors or managers who specialize in single-family residential projects.

In addition, check in at lumberyards that cater primarily to professionals (as opposed to the big-box retailers who sell mostly to weekend do-it-yourselfers) to build your list among their trade customers. Drive or walk the custom section of new housing developments and look for job-site signs of builders active in those neighborhoods.

From all of your sources, make notes about all of the contractors on your list as you add them, such as who referred them, how you found them, and why they made the list.

Narrowing the List

An easy way to winnow the contractors on your list is to look for repeat references from your sources and to rank or prioritize them based on the source of their referral or reason for being on the list. For instance, you may have liked the detailing on

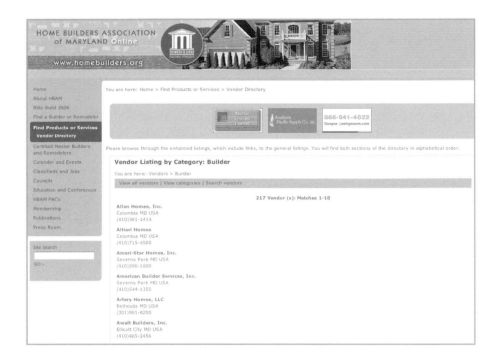

Online builder and contractor directories, occasionally offered through local home builders association Web sites, display a list of professionals (or member companies) from which you can usually obtain more information via Web site links, e-mail, or phone.

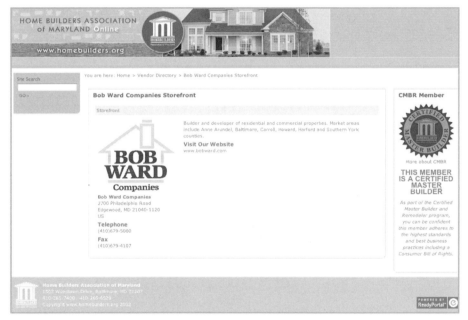

a custom home you saw (which may have matched similar detailing on the house plan you've selected), or you heard of a builder who managed the construction of a kit home or a house derived from a stock plan.

With that short list, conduct preliminary research online by visiting each builder's Web site, if he or she has one. Don't rule out a builder who does not maintain a Web site; instead, call the company and request a brochure or other marketing materials geared toward helping consumers make a thoughtful decision.

Whether you are reviewing materials online or in printed form, look for experience and finished homes that match up to your project and its location. A builder may advertise a partnership with a kit home or home plan supplier or showcase homes derived from those sources.

Look for past client references and testimonials and request contact information for them if you intend to follow up. Then take a look at the "Questions for References" sidebar above, refining the questions for your situation.

It may comfort you to investigate information about the company's approach to its customers and projects, how it manages the home-building process, and whether it offers project financing or partnerships with local lenders. Builders and contractors

increasingly offer this information either on a Web site, in a brochure, over the phone, or in face-to-face presentations.

Scope of work: Specific steps toward completion; the entire breadth of the project from start to finish.

Hiring Your Builder

Especially if you contact references, the preliminary research phase should narrow your list considerably, perhaps down to three or four candidates. The next step involves contacting and interviewing contractors directly.

Before you make those calls, prepare yourself with the questions you need to ask, and prepare for some questions *from* the contractor—namely, when you want to start or complete the project, whether the home will be a primary residence or vacation property, any work done to date (including the purchase of house plans and/or a kit package, as well as land), and how you found out about the builder. You probably won't be asked about your budget until the first face-to-face meeting, but be prepared with it, anyway . . . and be willing to share it when the time comes.

It's important to explain to each candidate that you are looking to negotiate a contract with one builder instead of going through a competitive bid process; some of the best builders refuse to bid jobs on the theory that clients simply evaluate each candidate by the estimate alone instead of less-tangible factors. Even so, make sure each candidate understands that you are conducting a competitive process *based* on those intangibles and that you have already calculated a budget and perhaps secured financing, depending on your lender's policies requiring a contractor agreement prior to loan approval.

Make sure, too, that candidates are aware that you have obtained plans from a house plan publisher, kit home company, or lumberyard. Offer a specific *scope of work* detailing what you need from a builder under those circumstances.

Schedule interviews with builders who have both the interest and the time to meet with you . . . and mark whether each arrives on time and prepared. That first meeting should be a conversation as much as an interview, and you should assess rapport as much as the builder's skills, experience, and interest. Decide beforehand what will impress you and what might dissuade you from hiring a candidate, and be ready to ask—and to probe for satisfactory answers to—the questions and issues that are important to you and your situation.

Assuming you'll interview three builders within a week's time, set and share with them a deadline for making a decision, with the possibility of follow-up calls or second meetings to aid that decision. Then stick to it. Selecting a contractor is a leap of faith that naturally causes hesitation, but trust your preparation and make a decision in a respectful and timely fashion and you'll set the stage for a solid relationship throughout the process.

The Construction Contract

Once you've made your selection, work with your builder to draft, refine, and sign a construction contract. The agreement should specify as much detail as possible about the scope of the project and your respective responsibilities, finances and payment process, subcontractor bidding and hiring practices, materials and products to be used in construction, lien releases and other protective measures, legal recourse, warranty procedures, and a schedule for completion.

In addition, a good contract outlines how and when you and your builder will communicate, be it scheduled meetings or weekly e-mails, job site walk-throughs and reviews, and change order management and documentation. More than any other factor, communication will either derail or ensure a successful project.

Your builder may have a standard contract that he or she may expect you to sign without alterations, but insist that the two of you review it, fill in any blanks, and customize it to your needs and your project. When it's to your satisfaction, hire a real estate attorney skilled in contracts or construction agreements to review the contract and red flag any concerns or open-ended issues.

The contract will likely dictate a schedule for payments. Make sure that payments, or *draws,* are tied to a specified phase of work or level of completion to your (and perhaps your lender's) satisfaction and according to the terms of the contract. You will likely be required to either make a deposit or pay a little up front upon signing the contract—typically no more than 10 percent of the total contract amount. This first draw often helps the builder *mobilize* or get the job site ready for the kit home package or helps him or her purchase the first batch of materials and cover the initial labor costs.

On the back end of the job, you'll likely have the last 10 percent of the contract amount left over to pay once you receive a certificate of occupancy (CO), which signals completion of the project in the eyes of the local building authority. You may negotiate, however, to hold some or all of that last payment until your builder completes a ***punch list*** of leftover items after you get final building code approval to move in. You can also bargain to reduce the up-front deposit and boost the last payment as an extra incentive for your builder to follow through if she has a history of letting the schedule slip.

Punch list: Items left to complete.

Pressure-treated wood: Lumber or other wood building products that have been treated with a chemical to resist rot, decay, and insect infestation; used when the wood product touches the ground.

The Construction Process

Part of the selection, negotiation, contract, and collaboration with your builder involves sharing your plans for obtaining blueprints and building materials through one or more of the catalog options available. Decisions and refinements made during that process have a huge influence over the type of construction and materials that will create your house as well as your budget and time frame for completion.

In fact, there are several ways and materials choices available to build the same house, especially if you purchase plans from a catalog and buy your materials from a local lumberyard, and even if you decide on a kit home package or a panelized prefab technique. While there are many efficient and increasingly common building innovations for home construction (see the "Building Options" section that follows), the *process* and *sequence* toward completion remain fairly universal (see the construction sequence on pages 55–59).

Whatever changes you make at this point will likely be among competitive materials choices and construction methods rather than design alterations, such as changes to the floor plan or roof pitch.

Every house, for instance, needs a foundation. House foundations are either monolithic slabs of poured concrete, raised floor or crawl spaces, or full basements. Poured concrete or concrete blocks (also called concrete masonry units, CMUs, or cinder blocks) are the most common materials used for residential foundations, though a small minority of builders use ***pressure-treated wood*** to build full basements.

Building any type of foundation requires excavation of the home site. Excavation may include clearing trees, shrubs, and other intrusions; grading the property or creating a building pad; and digging into the ground with a backhoe to accommodate the foundation's design and construction.

Rough-in: The various wires, cables, pipes, and other "behind the wall" conduits that bring services from a source (e.g., the main electrical panel) to locations in the house.

Joists: Floor or roof beams.

Structural framing follows the foundation, creating the home's skeleton that supports its plumbing, electrical, and other mechanical systems; its exterior and interior finishes; and its windows, chimneys, vents, and doors, among other components.

Frame construction is arguably the most dynamic phase of home building, in which there is daily progress and the home takes on a three-dimensional form. Using the most efficient structural systems, such as wall panels and roof trusses, the home's structural frame can be completed within a few days' time and be ready for windows, exterior finishes, and the initial installation (or *rough-in*) of various mechanical systems, insulation, and drywall.

Completion of the home's frame also includes roof and sidewall sheathing, in which panels of plywood or oriented strand board (OSB) are fastened to the exterior wall and roof frame and used as subflooring on the floor *joists.* Sheathing and subflooring provide a substrate for various finishes, namely your selections of siding, roofing, and flooring.

With the sheathing in place, your builder or the appropriate subcontractor prepares the window, door, and vent openings with flashing material to shed water and moisture away from the house. The entire roof is also protected with building paper (or "felt"), while the exterior sidewalls may feature foam insulation panels and/or a woven fiber sheeting, called house wrap or an air/vapor barrier, to further protect the wall framing from moisture intrusion and damage.

Most of today's windows and doors are prehung, which means that they are manufactured in a factory and delivered to the job ready to install in specified openings. Often a home's doors are installed near the end of construction to keep them safe from damage and vandalism; to "close up" and secure the house during the project, builders use (and reuse) low-grade construction doors in their place.

Building Options

Within this progressive sequence of so-called rough construction exist several options to boost productivity and quality while, ideally, lowering costs and saving time.

As a result, today's job sites showcase materials, components, systems, and even methods to speed, simplify, or combine framing and related tasks that most home buyers may find curious or worrisome. Rest assured, those outlined and explained here are reliable and durable, and they provide both builders and buyers with options for achieving housing goals. Turn to page 59 for details.

The construction sequence.

Step 1: Excavation. The lot is cleared and dirt is moved and leveled in preparation for the foundation. Excess or removed dirt is either hauled away or kept on-site for backfilling the foundation or for landscaping features, if necessary.

Step 2: Services. Every lot, whether in a subdivision (shown) or an individual home site, needs to be "improved" with basic services, such as electricity and water—at least stubbed up at the entrance to the lot for hook-up later—as well as perhaps streets, curbs, and gutters (also called infrastructure).

Step 3: Foundation. Typically built with poured concrete, the foundation provides a stable, level pad and structure for the house.

Step 4: Framing (delivery). The structural frame materials, typically lumber and other wood-based components, are delivered to the job site in phases and placed on the lot in close proximity to where they will be needed.

Step 5: Framing (installation). Whether built stick by stick or by using some variation of factory-built components, the structural frame stage is the most dynamic of the construction process, transforming two-dimensional plans into a three-dimensional, full-scale model within a few days or weeks.

Step 6: Windows and doors. Once the structural frame is sheathed with plywood or other panel product, the openings are fitted with windows and doors to enclose the structure. Flashing around the openings helps block water and air intrusion, saving energy and mitigating latent defects.

Step 7: Siding. Once the windows and doors are installed, the exterior finishes—such as the siding—go on, further protecting the structural frame and completing the overall design and appeal of the house.

Step 8: Roofing. Like the siding, the roofing is installed once the frame is sheathed and all openings are enclosed. A felt paper applied prior to the finished roofing (be that wood shakes, composite shingles, or tile, among others) helps shed water away from the roof structure. The application of the roofing and siding completes the shell of the house.

Step 9: HVAC and mechanicals. Once the structure is completely framed, the plumbing, electrical, heating and air, and other mechanical trade contractors install (or rough in) their respective systems.

Step 10: Insulation. Once the exterior shell is completed, or at least sheathed, contractors install insulating products in the walls, floors, and ceilings to retard thermal transfer through the structure.

Step 11: Drywall. Just as the exterior wall sheathing encloses the shell, drywall (or gypsum wallboard) is used to enclose the structural wall and ceiling cavities on the inside (wood sheathing is used on floors), containing the insulation and concealing the wiring and plumbing.

Step 12: Finishes. The drywall and floor sheathing (or subflooring) creates a "subfinish" or substrate for interior finishes, including flooring, paint, and wall coverings, as well as cabinets and plumbing and electrical fixtures.

Step 13: Paint. One of the last stages of construction is the application of interior paint, usually followed by installation of the finished flooring and the issuance of a certificate of occupancy (CO) that signals the home's completion.

Stick Framing

Since the advent of the sawmill, stick framing has been the predominant method for structural construction. Simply, all of the estimated framing lumber needed for wall *studs, headers, beams, rafters,* joists, *posts, plates,* and other applications is milled to dimensions (2×4, 4×4, 2×10, etc.) but is delivered to the job site in uncut lengths; the framing crew measures, cuts, and assembles the lumber according to the construction drawings and framing layout.

Studs: Wall framing.

Headers: Structural framing members above an opening (e.g., door or window).

Beams: Load-carrying, horizontal structural frame members.

Rafters: Structural members of the roof frame.

Posts: Load-carrying, vertical structural frame members.

Plates: Horizontal wood framing members placed between the foundation and the wall framing.

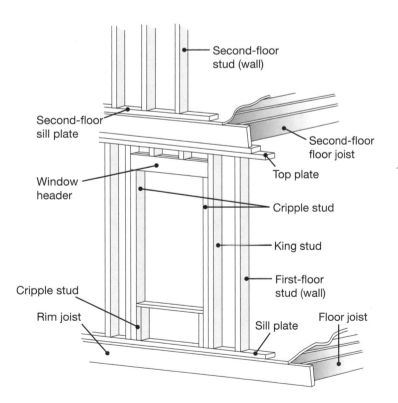

Second-floor stud (wall)

Second-floor sill plate

Window header

Cripple stud

Rim joist

Second-floor floor joist

Top plate

Cripple stud

King stud

First-floor stud (wall)

Sill plate

Floor joist

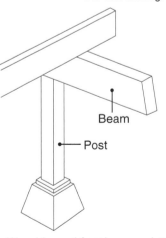

Beam

Post

Wood-based framing consists of several components, illustrated here; in stick framing, specifically, each component must be cut and fastened one at a time.

Stick framing requires a high level of carpentry skill and experience, including the ability to read blueprints and framing plans, make accurate cuts, and properly fasten the "sticks" together to create a secure and reliable structural frame.

As skilled construction labor continues to wane in both quantity and quality, especially among frame carpenters, stick framing increasingly results in substandard quality and a high percentage of wasted material due to miscuts and misuse. It also takes the most time among other framing options, a luxury that few builders, and a decreasing number of home buyers, can afford.

If you decide to purchase a home package from a lumberyard, you can either request an uncut load of framing materials for the plan you selected or, more likely, receive a load of precut materials to frame your chosen house. Most kit home suppliers also sell precut framing materials packages to speed construction, minimize lumber waste, and ensure that the kit is properly assembled.

Stick framing requires a high level of skill and several days of construction—luxuries that few home builders enjoy in modern housing production.

Precut Framing

A precut package is stick framing with the majority of the measurements and cuts already done at the lumberyard or kit home factory according to the framing plan for your chosen house design. Without the time and potential for materials waste, the framing crew can assemble and complete the home's structural frame faster and within the estimated materials budget. More than 31,000 precut home packages, excluding log and timber-frame kits, were shipped in 2000—a number that is expected to grow to 40,000 by 2010.

Precut framing packages, especially those from a kit home company, arrive with detailed instructions and a comprehensive list of the materials provided—perhaps to the point of numbered or labeled components similar to an Erector set. More often it will simply contain the requisite number and size of studs, headers, beams, and other framing components per the plans for the carpenters to assemble.

Though precut packages take away an often wasteful step in the framing stage (cutting lumber to length), they remain labor intensive and still require a high level of skill to be assembled properly. The precut components for log and timber-frame kits are often labeled to make them easier to identify their intended use, but precut packages from lumberyards using standard framing materials (or dimensional lumber) are likely to be less specific about which precut stud or beam goes where.

Engineered Lumber

Engineered lumber is a superior type of framing material compared to that milled from raw logs. Manufactured in sophisticated factories that reassemble wood fibers into a variety of structural members, engineered lumber delivers a higher level of *dimensional stability* and longer, stronger, and straighter lengths of material, enabling carpenters to use less wood (and thus spend less time) building a home's structural frame.

Unless part of a precut home package from a lumberyard or kit supplier, engineered lumber is typically delivered uncut. Even so, the pieces themselves are often obvious: *I joists,* for instance, cannot be mistaken for wall studs; beams cannot be field-cut into posts. The dimension and length of each piece of engineered lumber often dictates its use, though each will likely need to be cut to length on the job site according to the framing plans.

Engineered lumber has an environmental benefit. Using nontraditional and often smaller, faster-growing timber species than what's required to sawmill dimensional framing members, engineered lumber manufacturers reduce demand on increasingly restricted and unavailable forests harvested for lumber. The ability to use less material to build arguably a stronger structural frame reduces demand for raw timber.

Engineered I joists enable trade contractors to more easily weave plumbing and electrical systems through the structure.

Dimensional stability: The long-term ability of a structural framing member to remain straight and at its designed strength value.

I joists: I-shaped engineered floor beams.

Stronger and straighter than sawn lumber of the same dimension, engineered I joists create uniformly flat floor structures and span longer distances without support posts or columns intruding on the living spaces below.

Panelization: The use of factory-built structural framing components, including walls (or "panels"), roof trusses, and floor trusses.

Second-story platform: The "foundation" for a second story of a house.

Floor trusses: Engineered, factory-built floor beams.

Panelization and Component Framing

As the pressure increases to build homes faster without sacrificing quality while the number of skilled construction workers ebbs, many builders, lumberyards, and kit home suppliers have turned to factory-built framing components, also called *panelization.* Panelization accounted for more than 180,000 homes in 2000 and will be used for an estimated 200,000 homes by 2010.

Simply, instead of assembling a load of uncut or precut sticks on the job site, a crew of assembly-line workers builds sections of the home's walls, roof, and floor in a factory setting. The components are then loaded on a truck and delivered to the job site, craned into place, and secured to the foundation or *second-story platform.*

Traditionally, panelization has referred only to the walls of the house, but the term is often expanded to include all factory-built framing components. Other terms might be plated roof trusses or *floor trusses*—both of which achieve similar efficiencies to wall panels for home construction in their respective applications.

The primary advantage of factory-built components is a combination of speed and quality that appeals to all levels of home construction; the most affordable and most expensive homes built today both increasingly rely on component framing, proving their value in mainstream housing and debunking the reputation of prefabrication as a cheap alternative to stick-built methods.

Some of the nation's largest home-building companies, in fact, employ component framing, and a few to the extent of operating their own factories to supply their needs.

Building the major framing components in a factory—called panelization—and delivering them to the job site allows workers to assemble a house frame faster and with fewer mistakes and less wasted material.

A load of plated roof trusses, also built in a factory, will be craned into place to quickly create the roof structure.

About half of the largest lumberyards, meanwhile, operate component-framing facilities to serve builders and home package buyers, among more than 1,000 companies that operate huge, national or regional component manufacturing plants exclusively.

Faster construction and more reliable delivery and pricing from a factory not only hastens completion of the house but enables crews to close up the house (or *building envelope*) sooner, reducing the chance of damage from weather that can cause latent and costly problems in the finished home.

Recently, the Wood Truss Council of America, a building trade association, compared the construction of identical 2,600-square-foot homes, one a stick-framed house and the other built using factory components. The homes were constructed side-by-side to evaluate every stage of the framing process.

The results: Crews built the panelized house in one-third the time (about 250 fewer man-hours) and for less than half the labor cost, used 25 percent less lumber, and reduced materials waste by more than 75 percent. The total savings more than offset the slight premium cost for the engineered and prebuilt components compared to the cost of raw sticks, and it resulted in an overall cost reduction of nearly 20 percent. (Sears conducted a similar evaluation at the height of its *Modern Homes* catalog program, finding that its inclusive precut package reduced labor costs by 40 percent compared to the conventional home-building practices of the day.)

In the factory, engineering and computerized equipment culls the lumber for the highest grade and assembles it according to detailed plans and specifications—reducing the human element to supervision and troubleshooting, and resulting in a level of quality, performance, and reliability that perhaps even the best stick-framing

Building envelope:
A house that is "closed in" with its roofing, exterior siding, windows, and doors installed.

crew cannot match. To increase quality even more, some component manufacturers employ engineered lumber and steel framing members in their products.

Because panels and other framing components are built in sections instead of supplied as near-finished homes (as in a modular or manufactured home factory, see chapter 4), the system is flexible enough to accommodate almost any house design. Stock house plans are easily adapted to enable component framing, as are many kit packages, especially those sold through lumberyards with component-framing manufacturing capabilities.

Like kit home suppliers, lumberyards and panelizers realize that builders and home buyers can achieve even greater savings and efficiency if the framing components are either built or packaged with windows, doors, exterior finishes, drywall, and perhaps even a slew of interior finishes.

Modern component framing facilities include computerized operations for selecting and cutting lumber according to engineered plans. Long tables are used for assembling precut pieces into plated roof trusses, floor trusses, and wall panels, which are then rolled out to the shipping area.

Companies that preinstall windows and roughed-in mechanical systems in the wall sections at the factory are referred to as "closed panel" suppliers. Many prefab housing manufacturers use this system to deliver components that are almost complete to the job site, craning finished wall, floor, and roof panels into place and tying them together to complete the house. That method, however, is only one definition of the "prefab" segment, a general term that refers to a variety of factory-built housing types, including precut and panelized homes.

Most companies, however, provide "open panel" systems that package and ship, if not factory install, a variety of finish products along with the basic framing components, if only to avoid stricter transportation regulations and the hazards—including factory errors and potential damage—of shipping the near-complete wall, roof, and floor sections of a closed-panel system.

The more that's done in a factory, however, the faster the framing and other stages of construction once the components reach the job site. With an open-panel system and roof trusses, the shell of a one-story home can be completed in just a few days.

Prefab construction, a category of the factory-built housing segment, is often employed to create contemporary house styles, though the system can be used for almost any type of house design.

Alternative Framing Systems

Though component framing has already reached mainstream housing construction, some builders are trying even more innovative solutions to achieve greater efficiency.

Structural insulated panels (SIPs) and insulated concrete forms (ICFs) have emerged as legitimate if still somewhat fringe-level structural building systems. Both SIPs and ICFs further increase job-site productivity by combining structural components, assembly chores, and insulation into one solution.

Insulated concrete forms (ICFs, top row) and structural insulated panels (SIPs, bottom row) are two relatively new building technologies that combine multiple components to further reduce time and costs on the job site.

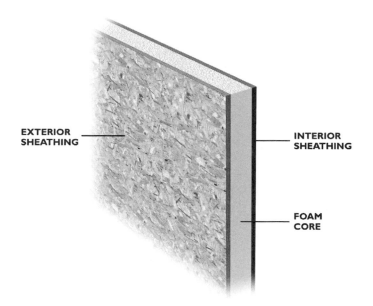

EXTERIOR
SHEATHING

INTERIOR
SHEATHING

FOAM
CORE

The cross-section of a structural insulated panel shows the structural members (the two outside panels) and the insulation (the core between the panels) that combine to produce a wall or roof section that is faster to assemble and provides greater energy efficiency than standard framing and insulating methods.

Specifically, SIPs are a combination of OSB sheathing panels sandwiching a layer of rigid foam insulation. The 4 × 8 foot or 4 × 10 foot sandwich panels are craned into place as exterior walls and roof-framing components, providing instant insulating value and nailing surfaces for exterior and interior finishes.

Forms: The molds in which concrete is poured to create walls, slabs, beams, and footings; also known as "formwork."

ICFs, meanwhile, provide instant and permanent insulating value to poured concrete walls. Molded from extruded foam, ICFs are extremely lightweight and fit together like Lego blocks to create the ***forms*** for the concrete foundation and above-grade walls; the cells of the foam blocks are filled with concrete just like CMUs or concrete formwork but are never stripped away once the concrete cures. The result is a concrete wall insulated on both the interior and exterior sides and done so in fewer steps than by conventional methods and materials.

SIP systems are designed to assemble quickly, creating the exterior walls and roof structure in a fraction of the time of stick framing and even less than open-wall component framing methods.

What's in a Kit?

When Sears and other catalog home sellers packaged their precut home kits during their heyday in the 1920s, the 30,000 pieces typically filled two railcars and required several trips from the train station to the home site. In addition to all of the necessary lumber, the package for the Chelsea model, for instance, included 750 pounds of nails, 22 gallons of paint and varnish, and 20,000 roof and sidewall shingles, among all of the essential finishes and perhaps even furniture and appliances. A seventy-five-page leather-bound book provided owner-builders with instructions for assembling the pieces.

Today's kit homes and home packages contain all of the necessary lumber, fasteners, and finishes needed (and instructions) to complete the home's structure. On average, new homes feature 19 windows and doors, 13,837 board feet of framing lumber, 12,123 square feet of sheathing material, 3,103 square feet of roofing, and 3,277 square feet of siding, among other essentials. That said, the kit home package might lack insulation, drywall, mechanical systems, and interior finishes—and certainly plumbing fixtures, appliances, and furniture—which you'll have to purchase and install (or hire others to install) to complete the house.

Like other forms of panelization, SIPs are made in a factory and shipped to the job site, where they are craned or lifted into place to create the walls and roof of the house.

Shipping a Kit

Kit home companies typically sell and ship their precut home packages within limited geographic areas or regions, making them inaccessible to buyers outside their shipping range. A few, however, operate nationally or even internationally, either by agreeing to ship anywhere (for a fee, of course) or contracting or operating satellite manufacturing facilities in strategic locations to serve a national consumer base and ship overseas. Local lumberyards, meanwhile, sell and ship their home packages within a much tighter geographic range, though the largest lumber-dealer chains operate dozens of outlets in various cities nationwide to serve customers in those markets with a similar mix of products, including home packages. Companies charge shipping costs (including insurance against damage) in different ways, from free delivery within a certain radius to extra for overseas, or they simply fold that cost into the price of the materials package. Shipping costs and availability may also depend on how easily the supplier can bring the materials or package to the building site; many require confirmation of adequate roads and clearances to ensure they don't get delayed or require another piece of equipment (such as a small crane or forklift) to make the delivery.

In addition to the potential construction efficiencies of both SIPs and ICFs, builders are attracted to both systems because they have proven to reduce latent construction defect problems in finished homes, such as drywall cracks and *nail pops,* and result in greater energy savings for home owners, compared to conventional (and even factory-built) framing schemes.

Nail pops: The heads of nails showing through a finished wall.

Prefabricated: Made or built elsewhere, typically in a factory.

The main hurdle for both systems is a higher building cost for materials and a labor force unfamiliar with their installation. It may cost 5 percent or more to build with SIPs compared to the cost of conventional stick framing, for instance, while concrete contractors typically charge a premium to install ICFs. Both systems still struggle to achieve local building code approval as well, if only because few inspectors and plan checkers are familiar with them.

Finishing the House

Unlike the foundation and especially the framing stages of construction, there is no industrialized system for finish work—unless you buy a manufactured home (see chapter 4). For kit homes and home packages as well, the efficiency of conventional methods is aided only by *prefabricated* building products and smart scheduling by the builder, general contractor, or construction manager.

Textured: Interior or exterior wall surfaces with an applied texture or pattern.

Typically builders will schedule the application of exterior finishes, such as roofing and siding, at the same time other contractors install the rough mechanicals, insulation, and drywall (in that order) inside the house. Once the drywall has been taped and *textured* (a process for concealing drywall panel seams and smoothing or adding texture to the wall surace), the walls and ceilings can be painted, wallpapered, paneled, or finished with another material.

The electrician, plumber, and heating contractor all return to finish their rough-ins installed during framing, from a dramatic entry chandelier to mundane (and multiple) towel hooks and vent register covers.

The finish process, including drywall taping and texturing, reduces the construction process to a pace that can be maddeningly slow. Not only does finish work require more precision and time, in contrast to the rough stages of excavation and framing, its progress is less dynamic and obvious. Even with a tight critical path, subcontractors often have to wait for those scheduled ahead of them to finish rather than work side-by-side, which stretches the schedule. You might not notice faceplates on outlets and switches that the electrician spent the bulk of the day installing. Or the electrician may be absent from the job site for a few days while the plumbers or drywall crew finish their work.

The last fixture installed in the house is the finished flooring, a requirement for a CO that signals the home is ready to occupy . . . even if the major kitchen appliances haven't arrived. Your builder will also complete outdoor features, such as decks and patios, and touch up, fix, or replace any mistakes or missing pieces.

Factory-Built Finishes

The efficiency of any building system, be it stick framing or panelization, is aided by the increasing industrialization of building products such as windows, doors, cabinets, plumbing fixtures, roofing, and siding, among several others.

In fact, almost all building materials are prefabricated and shipped to the job site by local, regional, and national suppliers ranging from low-tech sawmills to manufacturing facilities that rival NASA in their sophistication. Sears and other catalog home suppliers pioneered this kind of industrialization to enable them to provide complete building packages through the mail. Their legacy lives on in a supply chain for building products that affords increasing cost and time efficiencies on the job site.

Even with a CO in hand, or ideally before an official sign-off on the house by an outside inspector, you should insist on a final walk-through inspection with your builder before making your final payment.

Builders vary in their approach to final walk-throughs. Some, for instance, work to find and fix even the smallest detail before showing it to the owners and use the tour to simply educate owners about its operations and various systems; others use the walk-through as an opportunity to find and document punch-list items that require one or more service calls to repair, replace, or touch-up prior to and after move-in.

If you've maintained good communication with your builder or contractor throughout construction, nothing on the final walk-through should come as a surprise—especially his or her approach to the tour, which should be specified in the contract. Even if your builder seeks a zero-defect tour, be prepared to find something out of whack or not quite to your satisfaction. Ideally your builder will be equally prepared to address those minor requests.

A final walk-though inspection with your builder should be an opportunity to learn about the proper care and maintenance of your house and to agree on punch-list items that need to be addressed before or soon after move-in.

Costs and Payment

With all of the options available for selecting, altering, and building a home from a catalog, it would be impossible to estimate the costs of any given project. In its day Sears estimated that a painter would cost about $34.50 to finish a two-story model and a plasterer $200 to create the interior wall surfaces, among other contracted services, in addition to the $600 to $6,000 cost of the kit package itself; such estimates are more difficult in today's labor market.

The cost for your home is ultimately what's affordable according to your financial circumstances, as calculated in chapter 2. Except for the few examples of costs provided earlier to get you thinking, it would be futile and misleading for me to estimate or project all of the specific costs for your unique project. Instead, you should calculate specific costs for the various stages of planning for, purchasing, and completing your home.

Stock Home Plans

Home plans from a printed or online catalog are prepriced, as are many of the most common alterations. Custom changes are calculated by the plan service (occasionally for a fee, which is then credited toward your plan purchase, but nonrefundable if you decide not to buy the plans) or carry a separate charge if performed by your own design professional. Stock plan publishers accept checks and credit cards or secure online payment, and orders must be paid in full before they ship your plans.

Other costs include any additional documentation, such as materials reports, detail sheets, extra sets, and deck or landscape plans, as well as upgrades for vellum, reverse (which may also require a standard set so you can read the symbols and dimensions for reference), or custom reverse plans with legible markings. You'll also have to pay for shipping, though most plan sources offer a choice of mailing methods and costs.

Each set of plans is unique; even if you don't make any changes, the plans are generated or printed per your order. Therefore, plan publishers rarely accept returns or grant refunds. At best you'll receive partial credit for another purchase, assuming there's no evidence you've used the plans, but you may be forced to sacrifice the cost altogether. Vellums and reverse plans are typically nonreturnable or nonrefundable.

Kit Homes and Home Packages

Like conventionally built homes, kit homes and home packages are typically paid for by construction loans or other financing options detailed in chapter 2; at the very least you'll be required to put down a deposit to pay for the time and effort to create and refine your plans, then pay the balance before or soon after receiving the package.

Depending on the kit and how the materials are "staged" or shipped in progressive loads, you may be able to negotiate payments for each set of materials delivered. More likely the company will require you to cover the cost of manufacturing, materials, and shipping regardless of the pace of the delivery.

In addition to shipping (a cost most likely waived within a local lumberyard's or perhaps even a kit home's normal shipping radius), you may be expected to pay for equipment needed to crane and place the components into place. Usually a small crane can handle the job. Other costs may include permit fees for transporting materials across state lines or along interstate highways, insurance against stolen or damaged materials or components during their transportation and handling on-site, and the cost of a crane operator or truck driver. Make sure your homeowners insurance covers accidents or incidents related to construction by others on your property, and consider indemnifying yourself against claims from your contractor; in most states, he or she is required by law to carry liability insurance.

The most significant cost for either option—homes from a plan source or a kit home supplier—is labor. Again, with so many variables to consider, it's impossible to estimate or calculate what your specific labor costs may be. Even so, labor accounts for 50 percent of an average home's price, with the balance spent on land, materials, overhead and profit, and myriad fees.

Innovative building systems, such as component framing and SIPs, seek to trim labor costs by reducing on-site construction time and skill and perhaps the number of subcontractors and suppliers required as well as expenses related to financing and debt, insurance, defects and poor workmanship liability, and delays during the building process.

Warranty and Maintenance

House plans purchased from a catalog are designed to the latest national or regional building codes, but there's no guarantee or warranty that they will gain code approval through your local building department.

Plan publishers, therefore, recommend that a local structural engineer, architect, or licensed contractor review and amend your plans as necessary to meet the local building code regulations and permit requirements. Kit homes from outside the area will likely require a local certification, or "stamp," from a recognized professional before gaining code approval.

Once your house is finished, regardless of the system used, your builder and the team of subcontractors are responsible for defects in workmanship and systems for at least one year and any structural problems for at least two years, and probably longer. Some builders purchase warranty insurance that covers construction-related issues (as opposed to maintenance, which is the owners' responsibility) for ten or more years, though only a small percentage of home owner claims are ever justified, much less paid out. More often builders simply take care of the problem, occasionally defer the responsibility to a subcontractor or to the owners, or perhaps suffer the consequences of a lawsuit.

Negotiate or at least specify the terms of warranty services and responsibilities and document them in the contract. Keep records and all product-specific warranties from appliance and equipment manufacturers and subcontractors, as well as the contact information for whom to call for qualified warranty service. Learn the functions and operations of your new house and what you can do to maintain it and avoid problems . . . and litigation.

In many ways buying and building a home from a catalog mirror the traditional process of hiring an architect and a builder, getting materials from a lumberyard and other sources, and completing a wood-framed house.

But the various options and process of this housing type combine to deliver significant time and cost efficiencies from start to finish, maintaining the affordable, high-quality standards set by Sears and other mail-order catalog home companies a century ago.

Builders or representatives from subcontractors or suppliers on your project will schedule warranty service calls at your convenience to rectify issues or problems with products and systems.

Prefab homes, like the custom residence shown here, are only one segment of housing options available through catalogs and other printed and online resources.

Catalog of House Plan Publishers

The house plan publishers and services listed here include the industry's largest and well-known sources, but they represent a fraction of what's available. The World Wide Web has created an environment in which thousands of sources provide literally hundreds of thousands of house plans online. It would be impossible, and unnecessary, to list them all in this book.

For the most part, all of these house plan suppliers offer a wide range of home designs to suit just about any taste and budget. While the total number of plans offered by a particular source is an important consideration, a more critical measure is whether the source has a choice of house plans to match your needs.

To help narrow your options (and legwork), know up front what you need as specifically as possible. Before you contact a plan source (online, on the phone, or via e-mail), determine the number of bedrooms and bathrooms, the number of stories or levels, an estimated square footage, and the general style of the house, such as colonial or ranch. The more details you have up front, the easier it will be to narrow down not only the number of house plans to choose from but also the source of those plans.

The vast majority of house plan suppliers offer basic sets of plans (or blueprints) for a price usually less than $1,000 (often much less, depending on the square footage of the house). They also offer services to help modify the plans to suit your needs, location, and site conditions, typically on a per-hour fee basis. Because most house plans are altered slightly for construction, check into the publisher's terms and cost for making modifications.

Finally, a basic set of plans entitles (or licenses) you, the buyer, to build that house one time. If for some reason you want to build it more than once, many companies will accommodate that request by issuing and charging you for another license to use the same set of plans. If you think you might build the house more than once, check into the multiple-use terms and pricing of your house plan supplier.

House plan publishers distribute their plans nationwide, so there's no need to limit your choices to sources close to where you live or plan to build.

The best way to start the process is to dive in, especially online where these and other house plan sources offer easy, fast, and free ways to find the design and plan you need.

Note: "Additional information not provided by company" indicates that the company did not provide sufficient information to complete its listing.

Abbisoft House Plans, Inc.
17536 East Baker Place
Aurora, CO 80013
(800) 345–4663, (303) 671–6844;
fax (303) 671–7005
www.homeplanfinder.com
Year founded: 1994
Number of plans offered: 6,200
Price range (basic set): $300–
$1,000+
Price range (alterations): $65/hr.
Use restrictions: Multiple-time use
only with designer's permission

Ahmann Design
2202 Heritage Green Drive
Hiawatha, IA 52233
(800) 725–6852; fax: (319) 395–7933
www.ahmanndesign.com
Year founded: 1991
Number of plans offered: 2,000+
Price range (basic set): Starting at
$350 (single set); $0.20–$0.33/s.f. for
plans over 3,500 s.f.
Price range (alterations): Approx.
$60/hr.
Use restrictions: Depends on
plan/format; need additional
licenses for each house built

AmazingPlans.com
225 Atlantis Circle, Suite 101-A
St. Augustine, FL 32080
(800) 250–4505; fax: (904) 471–1714
www.amazingplans.com
*Additional information not
provided by company*

Architectural Designs
57 Danbury Road
Wilton, CT 06897
(800) 854–7852, (877) 229–2447
(USA & Canada)
(262) 521–4596 (international);
fax: (203) 761–8600
www.architecturaldesigns.com
Year founded: 1974
Number of plans offered: 6,272
Price range (basic set): $395–$7,000
(av. $650 per order)
Price range (alterations): $75/hr.
(av. $600–$700 per order)
Use restrictions: One-time use only

❖ Some plan sources print or
provide a pricing sheet for a
basic set of plans, while others
prefer to price each plan once

all modifications and other
selections (including extra
detail sheets) have been made.

Archway Home Plans
19 West Forty-fourth Street
New York, NY 10036
(800) 374–4766; fax: (212) 869–5215
www.archwaypress.com
Year founded: 1950
Number of plans offered: 700+
Price range (basic set): $400–$600
Price range (alterations): $65/hr.
Use restrictions: Reuse restrictions
and per-use cost (up to $250) per
designer; multiple-use licenses available

❖ Before applying for a building permit or starting construction of the house, consult a
local building permit office or
code official to determine if the
governing municipality requires
a review of your house plans.

**The COOL house plans
company**
4 Savannah Highway, Suite 15
Beaufort, SC 29906
(800) 482–0464, (843) 522–0699;
fax: (843) 522–0706
www.coolhouseplans.com
Year founded: 1997
Number of plans offered: 16,000+
Price range (basic set): $50
(sheds)–$6,000
Price range (alterations): $65/hr.
Use restrictions: Can build the same
plan up to ten times, depending on
plan and rights

Design Basics
11112 John Galt Boulevard
Omaha, NE 68137
(800) 947–7526, (402) 331–9223
(local); fax: (402) 331–5507
www.designbasics.com
Year founded: 1979
Number of plans offered: 1,900+
Price range (basic set): $700–$1,200
Price range (alterations): Quoted by
modification
Use restrictions: Unlimited use
rights

❖ House plans are generally
modified by the plan source to
meet national building codes,
but you'll still have to get them
approved by your local building
authority, which may require
some additional modifications
by a local architect, builder,
draftsperson, or engineer.

Design Evolutions Inc.
4132 Medlock River Court
Snellville, GA 30039
(866) 858–5133, (770) 761–5024
(metro Atlanta); fax: (770) 761–5024
www.designevolutions.com
Year founded: 1999
Number of plans offered: 130
Price range (basic set): $550–$1,950
Price range (alterations): $85/hr.
design time, $65/hr. drafting time
(average $500)
Use restrictions: One-time use only

❖ When you are ready to ask
for bids (or cost estimates) from
contractors or subcontractors,
you will need additional sets of
blueprints. Additional sets are
less expensive when ordered in
quantity with the original
order; make sure to order
enough blueprints for each of
the contractors to review and
provide a bid.

DesignHouse Inc.
234 North Magnolia Drive
Wiggins, MS 39577
(888) 909–7526, (601) 928–3234;
fax: (601) 928–7575
www.design-house.com
Year founded: 1990
Number of plans offered: 2,000+
Price range (basic set): Starting at
$350
Price range (alterations): Priced per
change requested
Use restrictions: One-time use only

Dream Home Source, Inc.
3275 West Ina Road, Suite 260
Tucson, AZ 85741
(800) 447–0027; fax: (800) 224–6699
www.dreamhomesource.com

Year founded: 1993
Number of plans offered: 15,000
Price range (basic set): $600–$1,200
Price range (alterations): Varies by type of alteration (average $2,200)
Use restrictions: One-time use only

❖ An increasing number of plan sources offer plans for building an apartment over a garage, which allows you to build a "temporary" house quickly so you can live on-site while your main house is under construction. The apartment can then be used as a guest suite, home office, or otherwise modified.

Frank Betz Associates, Inc.
2401 Lake Park Drive, Suite 250
Smyrna, GA 30080
(888) 717–3003, (770) 431–0888;
fax: (770) 435–7608
www.frankbetz.com
Year founded: 1976
Number of plans offered: 950+
Price range (basic set): Would not disclose
Price range (alterations): $195–$1,000 (prepriced list)
Use restrictions: One-time only for nonreproducible plans; multiple-use licenses available

❖ A custom architect or designer may charge as much as $10,000 to design a home and provide a full set of working drawings (blueprints), while a stock (or unchanged) plan from a home plan publisher often costs less than $2,000.

Global House Plans
(800) 645–1477; fax: (866) 491–9594
www.globalhouseplans.com
Year founded: 1980
Number of plans offered: 14,000+
Price range (basic set): Starting at $250
Price range (alterations): Starting at $50/hr.
Use restrictions: Depends on plan ordered

Hanley Wood Consumer Group
Customer Care Center
3275 West Ina Road, Suite 260
Tucson, AZ 85741-2152
(888) 846–8188; fax: (800) 224–6699
www.eplans.com
Year founded: 1946
Number of plans offered: 10,000
Price range (basic set): $750–$1,900
Price range (alterations): Varies by type of alteration (average $2,200)
Use restrictions: One-time use only

Homeplans.com
30700 Russell Ranch Road
Westlake Village, CA 91362
(888) 447–1946, (805) 557–2300;
fax: (805) 557–2680
www.homeplans.com
Year founded: 1946
Number of plans offered: 10,000+
Price range (basic set): $386–$1,000
Price range (alterations): Per job/request
Use restrictions: One-time use only

❖ A few online sources are Web portals to actual house plan suppliers, providing you with a list (or links) to those resources.

Home Plan Superstore
(800) 667–2231; fax: (866) 491–9594
www.weinmaster.com
Year founded: 1979
Number of plans offered: 14,000+
Price range (basic set): Starting at $250
Price range (alterations): Starting at $50/hr.
Use restrictions: Depends on plan ordered

Houseplans, Inc.
100 Rowland Way, Suite 300
Novato, CA 94945
(888) 596–4353; fax: (415) 878–4221
www.houseplans.com
Year founded: 1999
Number of plans offered: 19,000+
Price range (basic set): $600–$650 (average)
Price range (alterations): Starting at $150
Use restrictions: One-time use only; multiple-use licenses negotiated per designer

❖ Standard blueprint paper is a type of light-sensitive photographic paper (called diazo) commonly used for architectural plans. Vellum is a type of translucent paper that allows the lines of the floor plan to be erased so changes can easily be made to the plan.

Houseplansplus LLC
2200 Fowler Avenue, Suite C
Jonesboro, AR 72401
(877) 497–5267; fax: (870) 974–9401
www.houseplansplus.com
Year founded: 2002
Number of plans offered: 1,435
Price range (basic set): $600 (average)
Price range (alterations): Varies by designer
Use restrictions: Varies by designer/plan

National Home Planning Service, LLC
37 Mountain Avenue
Springfield, NJ 07081
(866) 798–3200, (973) 376–3200;
fax: (973) 376–6202
www.nationalhome.com
Year founded: 1948
Number of plans offered: 2,700
Price range (basic set): $375–$900 (single set)
Price range (alterations): Depends on plan/designer
Use restrictions: One-time use only; license available for multiple use

Parade of Home Plans
Haven Marketing Services, Inc.
11812 South Fifty-third Avenue
Papillion, NE 68133
(866) 299–3416, (402) 934–2601;
fax: (402) 934–2602
www.paradeofhomeplans.com
Year founded: 2003
Number of plans offered: 5,000+
Price range (basic set): Starting at $175
Price range (alterations): Depends on plan/designer
Use restrictions: Depends on plan/designer

The Plan Collection
P.O. Box 494
Logan, UT 84323-0494
(866) 787–2023, (435) 787–2023;
fax: (866) 422–8101
Year founded: 2001
www.theplancollection.com
Number of plans offered: 7,000+
Price range (basic set): $400–$3,000
Price range (alterations): Quoted by
designer
Use restrictions: One-time use only

❖ A reproducible set of plans
allows you to modify the plans
to meet your building codes,
climate conditions, and the land
(or lot) and enables a local
designer to make any design
changes. When you purchase a
reproducible master or vellum
set of plans (as opposed to
standard blueprints), you also
purchase a copyright release
that gives you the legal right to
modify and copy the original
design. Otherwise, the home
plan design is protected under
the terms of U.S. copyright law
and may not be copied or
reproduced in any way or by
any means.

PlanHouse, Inc.
P.O. Box 366
Brandon, MS 39043
(601) 939–2828; fax: (601) 932–4707
www.planhouse.com
Year founded: 1974
Number of plans offered: 700+
(plus contributing designers)
Price range (basic set): Starting at
$435
Price range (alterations): $55/hr.
Use restrictions: One-time use or
relicense at lesser fee for multiple
use

Rick Garner Designer
370 Towne Center Boulevard
Ridgeland, MS 39157
(877) 977–9485
www.rickgarner.com
Year founded: 1966
Number of plans offered: 300+
Price range (basic set): $450–$965
Price range (alterations): $75/hr.
Use restrictions: One-time use only

**The Sater Design
Collection, Inc.**
25241 Elementary Way, Suite 201
Bonita Springs, FL 34135
(800) 718–7526, (239) 495–5478;
fax: (239) 495–3735
http://dreamplans.com. www.sater
design.com
*Additional information not pro-
vided by company*

Scholz Design
3131 Executive Parkway
Toledo, OH 43606
(800) 627–6115; fax: (419) 531–6902
www.scholzdesign.com
*Additional information not
provided by company*

The Southern Designer
370 Towne Center Boulevard
Ridgeland, MS 39157
(877) 737–5267
www.southerndesigner.com
Year founded: 2001
Number of plans offered: 3,000+
Price range (basic set): $150–$3,000
Price range (alterations): No modifi-
cations offered
Use restrictions: One-time use only

❖ Some of the largest house
plan publishers partner with
lumberyards and building materials chains to offer their plans
through local retail outlets;
the lumberyard or home center
typically ensures the plans will
meet local building code
requirements.

Catalog of Kit Homes and Home Packages

The world of kit homes and home packages includes a variety of suppliers, from companies solely dedicated to producing and delivering complete house kits that home owners and builders assemble on-site to local lumberyards that marry their lumber and building materials with in-house design services to create home packages for consumers and contractors.

The kit home and/or home package suppliers listed here are primarily the former: modern versions of the Sears Catalog Home model of the early twentieth century and the recognized leaders in that niche of the home-building industry based on sustained histories, a growing realm of available plans and packages, and dedication to the kit home concept. To list every lumberyard that offers some sort of home package would be unwieldy and unnecessary, as all of them operate within their respective local markets and rarely, if ever, ship materials (much less entire home packages) beyond that geographic radius.

The information about the companies listed below includes not just where they are headquartered but, more important, in which states they supply their kit home packages. As you consider this option for your new home, your first priority is to match the location of the house you want to build (especially if it is in a different city or state than your current home) with a company that supplies that location. For a list of companies by state and sales territory, see page 85,

The listings include some insight into the company's history, specifically years in business, which is one indicator of a legitimate and reliable supplier in this particular industry.

In addition, each company is listed with the type (or types) of building system it offers, whether it's panelized, timber frame, logs, or another building method or material. While panelized homes typically offer the most housing design choices, from Cape Cod to ranch, companies that specialize in timber-frame and log homes are best suited to supply those housing styles.

Finally, it may be important for you to know if the company offers a printed or electronic catalog of its available (or "stock") house designs, which may include a planning guide and/or a detailed explanation of the building system (such as panelization). Companies differ on whether they charge a nominal fee for their catalog/guidebooks, just as they differ on whether to charge extra for the cost of design services or house plans above and beyond the cost of the actual kit home package of materials. Once you narrow your choices to a few potential suppliers, get more detail about whether the cost of plans is included in the materials package and, if so or not, how that policy includes any limitations or penalties for violating it.

Like any business, kit home and home package suppliers are increasingly sophisticated in their marketing and sales efforts. Most, for instance, maintain Web sites that provide an ever-evolving amount of information about the company and the industry. Once you've found the companies that supply the location of your new home, get online first to start winnowing your choice of a building partner.

Note: "Additional information not provided by company" indicates that the company did not provide sufficient information to complete its listing.

American Ingenuity, Inc.
8777 Holiday Springs Road
Rockledge, FL 32955-5805
(321) 639–8777; fax: (321) 639–8778
www.aidomes.com
Year founded: 1976
Sales territory: Nationwide
Building system: Geodesic domes
Plan catalog available? Yes
Cost of plans included in materials package? No

American Standard Building Systems, Inc.
700 Commerce Court
P.O. Box 4908
Martinsville, VA 24115
(800) 888–4908; fax: (276) 638–3983
www.ownerbuildersolutions.com
Year founded: 1968
Sales territory: International
Building system: Panelized
Plan catalog available? Yes
(online only)
Cost of plans included in materials package? Typically refunded upon final delivery of house package

AmeriPanel Homes Corporation
102 Northeast Second Street, #262
Boca Raton, FL 33432
(800) 678–2183; fax: (800) 678–2248
www.ameripanel.com
Year founded: 1999
Sales territory: International
Building system: Panelized
Plan catalog available? Yes
Cost of plans included in materials package? Yes

Armstrong Lumber Company, Inc.
2709 Auburn Way North
Auburn, WA 98002
(800) 868–9066; fax: (253) 833–5878
www.armsystem.net
Year founded: 1952
Sales territory: International
Building system: Panelized; framing components
Plan catalog available? Yes
Cost of plans included in materials package? No

Beaver Mountain Log & Cedar Homes, Inc.
200 Beaver Mountain Drive
Hancock, NY 13783-9708
(609) 467–2700; fax: (607) 467–2715
www.beavermtn.com
Year founded: 1982
Sales territory: Northeastern USA (CT, MA, ME, NC, NH, NJ, NY, OH, PA, RI, VA, VT, WV) and International

Building system: Panelized timber frame; log homes
Plan catalog available? Yes
(planning guide: $18.95)
Cost of plans included in materials package? Yes

❖ In 1908 Frank W. Kushel, the manager of Sears's china department, was assigned to eliminate the company's unprofitable building materials mail-order business. Instead he created the *Honor-Bilt Modern Homes* catalog that included 22 precut houses priced from $650 to $2,500. Eventually the biannual catalogs offered 450 house selections. Through 1940 (when the division shut down), Sears sold an estimated 75,000 homes through its catalogs.

Built On Integrity (B.O.I.), Inc.
P.O. Box 62338
Boulder City, NV 89006
(702) 294–2525; fax: (702) 294–2531
www.spaceconstruction.com
Additional information not provided by company

Carolina Model Home Corporation/Regal Industries, Inc.
605 German Street
Fayetteville, NC 28301
(800) 272–4404; fax: (910) 223–1333
www.gotohomeworks.com
Additional information not provided by company

Classic Post & Beam
Division of Northeastern Log Homes
P.O. Box 546
York, ME 03909
(800) 872–2326; fax: (207) 363–2411
www.classicpostandbeam.com
Additional information not provided by company

Clever Homes, LLC
665 Third Street, Suite 400
San Francisco, CA 94107
(415) 344–0806; fax: (415) 344–0807
www.cleverhomes.net
Additional information not provided by company

Deltec Homes, Inc.
69 Bingham Road
Asheville, NC 28806
(800) 642–2508; fax: (828) 254–1880
www.buildingsmart.net
Additional information not provided by company

Doubletree Homes & Development, Inc.
52288 Highway 93
Ronan, MT 59864
(406) 675–8733; fax (406) 675–8734
www.doubletreehomes.com
Additional information not provided by company

❖ Sears's 3,000-square-foot "Magnolia" plan, introduced in 1918, featured 8 rooms, 2.5 baths, second-floor roof terraces, and a side porte cochere; the package sold for $5,140.

Eagle's Nest Homes, Inc.
205 Eagle's Nest Drive
Canton, GA 30114
(800) 579–1079; fax: (770) 720–7605
www.eaglesnesthomes.com
Year founded: 1983
Sales territory: International
Building system: Panelized
Plan catalog available? Yes
Cost of plans included in materials package? Yes (first set)

EZ Home Kits
2820 Audubon Village Drive, #186
Audubon, PA 19403
(800) 886–9369
www.ezlogkits.com
Additional information not provided by company

FarWest Homes
Division of West Coast Mills, Inc.
P.O. Box 480
Chehalis, WA 98532
(800) 752–0500, (360) 748–3351;
fax: (360) 748–6443
www.farwesthomes.com
Year founded: 1947
Sales territory: AK, CA, ID, OR, WA, plus export
Building system: Panelized
Plan catalog available? Yes
Cost of plans included in materials package? Yes

FischerSIPS, Inc.
1843 Northwestern Parkway
Louisville, KY 40203
(800) 792–7477; fax: (502) 778–0508
www.fischersips.com
Year founded: 1986
Building system: Structural insulated panels (SIPs)
Additional information not provided by company

❖ House plan publishers typically offer a combination of designs from an in-house staff of architects or designers as well as designs from independent design professionals. Some sources are simply brokers for several independent architects, each perhaps with slightly different terms for making alterations or authorizing multiple uses of the same plan.

Forest Homes
Route 522 Road 1
Box 131K
Selinsgrove, PA 17870-9782
(570) 374–0131; fax: (570) 374–6093
www.foresthomes.com
Year founded: 1976
Sales territory: CT, DC, DE, GA, MA, MD, ME, MI, NC, NH, NJ, NY, OH, PA, RI, SC, VA, WV

Building system: Panelized
Plan catalog available? Yes
Cost of plans included in materials package? Yes

Freespan Homes, Inc.
Castle Town Square North
4290 Route 8
Allison Park, PA 15101
(888) 466–5803; fax: (412) 486–9368
www.freespanhomes.com
Year founded: 1997
Sales territory: Nationwide
Building system: Panelized (wood); precut/pre-engineered steel
Plan catalog available? Yes (by request)
Cost of plans included in materials package? Yes (for standard plans)

Global Panel Solutions, LLC
6433 Topanga Canyon Boulevard, Suite 432
Canoga Park, CA 91303
(818) 332–1440; fax: (818) 710–1952
www.globalpanelsolutions.com
Year founded: 2003
Sales territory: International
Building system: Panelized
Plan catalog available? No (custom design)
Cost of plans included in materials package? Both (negotiated)

Harvest Homes, Inc.
185 Railroad Avenue
Delanson, NY 12053
(518) 895–2341; fax: (518) 895–2287
www.harvesthomes.com
Year founded: 1960
Sales territory: CT, MA, ME, NH, NJ, NY, PA, RI, VT
Building system: Panelized
Plan catalog available? Yes (printed and CD-ROM)
Cost of plans included in materials package? No

❖ A leather-bound book accompanying a package of twenty-five to thirty tons of materials instructed Sears home owners regarding the assembly of their home and included the caveat: "Do not take anyone's advice as to how this building should be assembled."

Hearthstone, Inc.
1630 East Highway 25/70
Dandridge, TN 37725
(800) 247–4442; fax: (423) 397–9262
www.hearthstonehomes.com
Year founded: 1970
Sales territory: International
Building system: Timber frame; logs; structural insulated panels (SIPs)
Plan catalog available? Yes
Cost of plans included in materials package? Yes

Hive Modular
1330 Quincy Street NE, Suite 306
Minneapolis, MN 55415
(612) 379–4382; fax: (612) 331–4638
www.hivemodular.com
Additional information not provided by company

Idaho Pre-Cut Homes
P.O. Box 665
Emmett, ID 83617
(208) 365–1134 (southwestern Idaho), (800) 764–2601 (all other areas); fax: (208) 365–1135
www.idahoprecuthomes.com
Year founded: 1992
Sales territory: Western United States (AZ, CA, CO, ID, MT, NM, NV, OR, TX, UT, WA, WY)
Building system: Panelized
Plan catalog available? Yes
Cost of plans included in materials package? No

❖ The term "modern home" was part of early-twentieth-century vernacular to describe a house with centralized heating, electricity, and indoor plumbing.

Insulspan, Inc.
9012 East U.S. Highway 223
P.O. Box 38
Blissfield, MI 49228
(517) 486–4844; fax: (517) 486–2056
www.insulspan.com
Additional information not provided by company

KitHaus
15952 Strathern Street
Van Nuys, CA 91406
(310) 889–7137; fax: (310) 440–9563
www.kithaus.com
Additional information not provided by company

Landmark Home & Land Co., Inc.
405 Johnson Road, Suite 2
P.O. Box 9118
Michigan City, IN 46361
(800) 830–9788; fax: (800) 964–2821
www.frameahome.com
Year founded: 1991
Sales territory: Lower 48
Building system: Panelized
Plan catalog available? No
Cost of plans included in materials package? Yes

Lindal Cedar Homes
Box 24426
Seattle, WA 98124
(800) 426–0536; fax: (206) 725–1615
www.lindal.com
Year founded: 1945
Sales territory: International
Building system: Custom precut
Plan catalog available? Yes
Cost of plans included in materials package? Yes

Marmol Radziner Prefab
12210 Nebraska Avenue
Los Angeles, CA 90025
(310) 689–0089; fax: (310) 826–6226
www.marmolradzinerprefab.com
Additional information not provided by company

Multi-Facetted Homes
HCR-3 Box 11110
Keaau, HI 96749-9226
(808) 982–6647; fax: (808) 982–5210
www.multi-facettedhomes.com
Year founded: 1988
Sales territory: International
Building system: Panelized shells
Plan catalog available? Brochure package with floor plan sheets
Cost of plans included in materials package? Discounted

Natural Spaces Domes, Inc.
37955 Bridge Road
North Branch, MN 55056
(800) 733–7107; fax: (651) 674–5005
www.naturalspacesdomes.com
Year founded: 1978
Sales territory: International
Building system: Precut components for dome-shaped homes
Plan catalog available? Yes
Cost of plans included in materials package? No

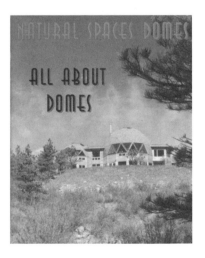

New Community Technologies, Inc.
233 West Market Street
Newark, NJ 07103
(973) 639–7861; fax: (973) 623–3612
Additional information not provided by company
*Additional information not
provided by company*

Normerica Building Systems
150 Ram Forest Road
Gormley, ON L0H 1G0 Canada
(800) 361–7449; fax (905) 841–9061
www.normerica.com
Year founded: 1980
Sales territory: International
Building system: Post and beam;
timber frame; wall and roof panels
(complete shell)
Plan catalog available? Yes
Cost of plans included in materials
package? Yes

Norse Building Systems
1100 Barnett Road
Ladysmith, WI 54848
(715) 532–0600; fax: (715) 532–0660
www.norsehomes.com
*Additional information not pro-
vided by company*

**Northern Design and Building
Associates, Ltd.**
P.O. Box 47
Hudson Falls, NY 12839
(800) 576–0557; fax: (518) 747–8032
www.northerndesign.com
Year founded: 1993
Sales territory: Maine to Virginia
Building system: Panelized
Plan catalog available? Yes (samples
of custom and some stock plans)
Cost of plans included in materials
package? Yes

Original Lincoln Logs Ltd.
5 Riverside Drive
P.O. Box 135
Chestertown, NY 12817
(800) 833–2461, (518) 494–5500;
fax: (518) 494–7495
www.lincolnlogs.com
Year founded: 1977
Sales territory: International
Building system: Log homes;
panelized; cedar
Plan catalog available? Yes ($12)

Cost of plans included in materials
package? Yes (includes engineering)

Riverbend Timber Framing
P.O. Box 26
Blissfield, MI 49228
(517) 486–4355; fax: (517) 486–2056
www.riverbendtf.com
*Additional information not pro-
vided by company*

R-Valued Homes, Ltd.
490 North Main Street, #127
Wasilla, AK 99654
(907) 357–2769; fax: (907) 357–2770
www.rvaluehomes.com
*Additional information not
provided by company*

Shelter Systems Limited
633 Stone Chapel Road
Westminster, MD 21157
(410) 876–3900; fax: (410) 857–5754
www.sheltersystems.com
*Additional information not pro-
vided by company*

SmartStart Building Systems
16 William F. Palmer Road
Moodus, CT 06469
(888) 873–1970, (860) 873–9294;
fax: (860) 873–9940
www.smartstartbuildingsystems.com
Year founded: 1999
Sales territory: CT, DE, MA, MD, ME,
MI, NC, NH, NY, OH, PA, RI, SC, VA,
WV
Building system: Panelized
Plan catalog available? Yes
Cost of plans included in materials
package? Yes

Sterling Homes, Inc.
111 Boston Post Road, Suite 106
Sudbury, MA 01776
(978) 579–9833; fax: (978) 443–8139
www.sterlingh.com
*Additional information not pro-
vided by company*

❖ Using wall panels instead
of stick framing saves an estimated 30 percent of labor and
materials costs and generates
20 percent less lumber waste,
according to *Automated
Builder* magazine (December
2004).

Taalman Koch Architecture
2404 Wilshire Boulevard, Suite 11F
Los Angeles, CA 90057
(213) 380–1060; fax: (213) 380–1260
www.tkithouse.com
*Additional information not pro-
vided by company*

Timberline Geodesics
2015 Blake Street
Berkeley, CA 94704
(800) 366–3466; fax: (510) 849–4481
www.domehome.com
Year founded: 1968
Sales territory: Nationwide
Building system: Geodesic dome
(hub and strut)
Plan catalog available? Yes
Cost of plans included in materials
package? No

**Topsider Building
Systems, Inc.**
P.O. Box 1490
Clemmons, NC 27012
(336) 766–9300; fax: (336) 766–1110
www.topsider.com
*Additional information not pro-
vided by company*

Woodmaster Foundations, Inc.
P.O. Box 66
Prescott, WI 54021
(800) 584–9585; fax: (715) 262–5079
www.wfionline.com
*Additional information not
provided by company*

Woodsmen Midwest, Inc.
669 Southwest Fifteenth Street
Forest Lake, MN 55025
(651) 464–2900; fax: (651) 222–3195
*Additional information not pro-
vided by company*

Yankee Barn Homes, Inc.
131 Yankee Barn Road
Grantham, NH 03753
(603) 863–4545; fax: (603) 863–4551
www.yankeebarnhomes.com
Year founded: 1968
Sales territory: International
Building system: Panelized
Plan catalog available? Yes (2; plan-
ner books, including sample plans)
Cost of plans included in materials
package? Yes (plans not sold separately)

Kit Homes and Home Packages by State and Sales Territory

ARKANSAS
R-Valued Homes, Ltd.

CALIFORNIA
Global Panel Solutions, LLC (panelized; international)
Timberline Geodesics (geodesic dome [hub and strut]; nationwide)

CONNECTICUT
SmartStart Building Systems (panelized; serving CT, DE, MA, MD, ME, MI, NC, NH, NY, OH, PA, RI, SC, VA, WV)

FLORIDA
American Ingenuity, Inc. (geodesic domes; nationwide)
AmeriPanel Homes Corporation (panelized; international)

GEORGIA
Eagle's Nest Homes, Inc. (panelized; international)

HAWAII
Multi-Facetted Homes (panelized shells; international)

IDAHO
Idaho Pre-Cut Homes (panelized; serving AZ, CA, CO, ID, MT, NM, NV, OR, TX, UT, WA, WY)

INDIANA
Landmark Home & Land Co., Inc. (panelized; serving the continental United States)

KENTUCKY
FischerSIPS, Inc. (structural insulated panels/SIPs)

MAINE
Classic Post & Beam

MARYLAND
Shelter Systems Limited

MASSACHUSETTS
Sterling Homes, Inc.

MICHIGAN
Insulspan, Inc.

MINNESOTA
Natural Spaces Domes, Inc. (precut components for dome-shaped homes; international)
Woodsmen Midwest, Inc.

MONTANA
Doubletree Homes & Development, Inc.

NEVADA
Built On Integrity (B.O.I.), Inc.

NEW HAMPSHIRE
Yankee Barn Homes, Inc. (panelized; international)

NEW JERSEY
New Community Technologies, Inc.

NEW YORK
Beaver Mountain Log & Cedar Homes, Inc. (panelized timber frame; log homes; serving CT, MA, ME, NC, NH, NJ, NY, OH, PA, RI, VA, VT, WV, international)
Harvest Homes, Inc. (panelized; serving CT, MA, ME, NH, NJ, NY, PA, RI, VT)
Northern Design and Building Associates, Ltd. (panelized; serving ME to VA)
Original Lincoln Logs Ltd. (log homes; panelized; cedar; international)

NORTH CAROLINA
Carolina Model Home Corporation/Regal Industries, Inc.
Deltec Homes, Inc.
Topsider Building Systems, Inc.

❖ When searching for a plan online, check out the increasing variety of aftermarket items, including furniture planners and stencils you can apply to the set of house plans you select.

PENNSYLVANIA
EZ Home Kits
Forest Homes (panelized; serving CT, DC, DE, GA, MA, MD, ME, MI, NC, NH, NJ, NY, OH, PA, RI, SC, VA, WV)
Freespan Homes, Inc. (panelized [wood]; precut/pre-engineered steel; nationwide)

TENNESSEE
Hearthstone, Inc. (timber frame; logs; structural insulated panels/SIPs; international)

VIRGINIA
American Standard Building Systems, Inc. (panelized; international)

WASHINGTON
Armstrong Lumber Company, Inc. (panelized; framing components; international)
Farwest Homes (panelized; serving AK, CA, ID, OR, WA, and export)
Lindal Cedar Homes (custom precut; international)

WISCONSIN
Norse Building Systems
Woodmaster Foundations, Inc.

CANADA
Normerica Building Systems (post and beam; timber frame; wall and roof panels; international)

A modern manufactured home factory is a complex and often computerized assembly line in which several homes (and sections of homes) are in various stages of construction at the same time.

CHAPTER 4

Homes from a Factory

MOST OF THE MATERIALS USED to site build a single-family home, from roof trusses to windows and siding, are actually produced in manufacturing facilities and assembled on the job site to create a finished home. But a large segment of the housing industry brings the materials together and puts them on an assembly line to provide near-complete homes from a factory. Simply, so-called factory-built housing puts a significant percentage of the construction process under one roof and away from the job site. Instead of relying on a collection of trade contractors to assemble all the pieces on your building location individually, such homes are built by a team of factory workers, often in less time and to a higher standard of quality than site-built homes.

Beginning as trailer coaches in the 1920s and popularized by sleek, silver Airstream trailers following World War II, the mobile home industry divided itself by the mid-1970s: one side became what is now known as recreational vehicles and so-called fifth-wheel trailers, while the other became manufactured, or HUD-code, housing.

Today the latter represents a $10 billion-a-year industry that houses more than 22 million Americans and builds up to one-fifth of all new homes annually. Shipments of manufactured homes increased at a greater rate compared to all housing sales in the United States between 1990 and 2000, primarily in the South, and peaked in

Be sure to refer to the extensive catalogs of manufactured and modular home suppliers, as well as the list of the industry's national trade associations, provided at the end of this chapter. You'll find helpful hints about using the catalog to narrow your choices.

Trailer coaches of the early to mid-twentieth century were the precursors to an industry of manufactured homes as well as recreational vehicles and modern fifth-wheel trailers.

The manufactured housing industry has evolved from wheeled homes to modern, permanent structures that are considered real property and indistinguishable from site-built homes.

1998 with nearly 375,000 homes sold nationwide. Owners run the gamut from first-time home buyers to retirees and second-home buyers, with a near-even distribution among age groups.

Industry maturation and widespread popularity aside, many people maintain a perception about manufactured housing as rusty, tin-sided, 12-foot-wide trailers set in rows along a shared driveway. It's a persona the industry may never shed, despite the fact that modern manufactured homes (and, to an even greater extent, modular homes; see "The Modular Difference" sidebar later in this chapter) bear only a slight

Also Known As

Amendments to the National Mobile Home Construction and Safety Standards Act in 1980 included a decree that the industry regulated by the law was to be known as "manufactured housing." However, by habit and reputation, marketing, and even some mystery, the industry enjoys (some say suffers from) a variety of names. Any one of the following terms, occasionally used in combination, mean essentially the same thing:

Manufactured home
HUD-code home
Factory-built home
Mobile home
Trailer home
Off-site home (or off-site construction)
Single-wides/double-wides

resemblance to their predecessors in older mobile home parks. If this chapter weren't devoted to houses from a factory, you may never have known that the completed homes pictured here were in fact "mobile" homes transported by big rigs from a factory to a building site.

Part of the industry's inability to rid itself of the negative mobile home image and label is that manufactured housing still provides the bulk of low-cost, for-sale housing for low-income families in this country. In 2001 the average *multisection* HUD-code home sold for $55,100, about one-third the average cost to construct a site-built home, not counting the price of land and other fees and expenses for either type. On an average *square-foot basis,* manufactured homes are less than half the cost of their built-on-site counterparts.

The challenge facing the manufactured housing industry is that too many people equate affordability with a cheap and low-quality product. By design and construction, however, manufactured homes perform every bit as well as, and sometimes better than, traditionally built houses.

Built to a set of national codes and standards called the HUD code (see the "What's the HUD Code?" sidebar), which matches up favorably to building codes enforced by any local municipality, manufactured homes employ comparable materials and systems—including wall studs, insulation, finished roofing, and textured walls, as well as energy-saving features and systems—to those assembled into site-built homes. An increasing number achieve (or can be manufactured to meet) federal *Energy Star* standards. There's truly very little difference in quality between comparably sized homes built in a factory and those constructed on-site.

As a result of quality construction and advances in overall design and detailing, manufactured housing has managed to gain a small foothold among second-home buyers who are motivated by time savings as much or more so than a bottom-line benefit. Buy a home from a factory and you'll move in within three months, and possibly less. That reduces a lot of the time and hassle of building a second home in a secluded vacation spot.

Multisection: More than one section (e.g., "double-wide").

Square-foot basis: A method for calculating costs based on a square foot of area; also known as "per-square-foot basis."

Energy Star: A federal program that sets standards for the energy use of a variety of consumer products (www.energystar.gov).

Living areas and kitchens in today's manufactured homes offer the same comfort and convenience as any site-built home.

The vast majority of manufactured homes, in fact, are placed (or set) in rural areas on private and scattered home sites. Meanwhile, HUD-code home subdivisions, akin to other new-home neighborhoods, currently account for only 10 percent of the market but are gaining political and social favor as in-town alternatives to the mobile home parks of the past.

Though still built with a wheeled chassis for shipping purposes, the majority of modern manufactured homes are placed on permanent foundations in suburban communities, with site-built garages and other features that put them on par with traditional housing.

There are subtle yet important distinctions between manufactured and site-built homes that will influence your decision to choose this type of housing, including how they are sold and shipped (the latter influencing design decisions as well), what needs to be done (and by whom) to prepare the building site for the home's delivery and placement, and financial options and prejudices that may hinder the home-buying process.

Study these and other differences carefully and weigh your priorities and circumstances against the various limitations and benefits afforded by manufactured homes.

What's the HUD Code?

In the late 1960s and early 1970s, as people began to use tow-behind trailer homes more as permanent residences and less as recreational vehicles that moved with them, the industry and the federal government recognized the need to regulate manufacturing standards for mobile homes. The enactment of the National Mobile Home Construction and Safety Standards Act in 1976, better known as the HUD code (so named for the law's enforcement agency, the U.S. Department of Housing and Urban Development, or HUD), recognized and regulated the division between recreational vehicles and a new type of single-family housing: the manufactured, or mobile, home. As such, the new law established the first national building code—a standard that all HUD-code home manufacturers must meet with every house they build, certified as such by a third-party inspector before shipping. In 1980 Congress amended the HUD code to officially recognize mobile homes as buildings instead of vehicles or trailers while also mandating an official (if not publicly enforced) name change to "manufactured housing" to replace the outdated and arguably less accurate "mobile home" moniker. In 2000 the Manufactured Housing Improvement Act ensured more timely and systematic updates to the HUD code to account for industry innovation and advances in factory construction technology.

The Modular Difference

Manufactured, or HUD-code, homes are not the only type of housing built primarily in a factory. Modular homes are a fast-growing segment of the housing industry that also employ assembly-line production, but in accordance with conventional building codes regulated by the states and municipalities in which the homes are eventually located. That key difference enables modular home manufacturers to build multistory (as well as multisectional) homes that appear even more like site-built houses. Unlike panelized framing systems that speed on-site construction, modules arrive as near-complete homes from the factory, including interior and exterior finishes. Another difference between modular homes and manufactured homes is that the former are sold almost exclusively to developers and builders instead of directly to the general public, making the sales process more akin to site-built homes. The modular industry attracts builders and developers looking for a turnkey, off-site building alternative to a traditional site-built construction process, saving them an even more significant amount of time and money than panelization, from the moment they buy land to when they can deliver finished homes.

Investigating the Market

If a manufactured home intrigues you for whatever reason, it's important to understand the buying process and its distinct differences from any other type of home purchase.

Manufactured home sales centers are becoming more sophisticated in their marketing efforts by placing model homes in neighborhood settings.

Manufactured home builders operate similarly to automakers. In addition to building their products in a factory, they sell their homes from roadside sales centers. A dealer, also called a builder or retailer, will likely have a few *model homes* available to tour to get a sense of the features you can expect from the company or companies she represents; a salesperson may even entice you to buy what's on the lot at a reduced price instead of ordering your home from the factory.

Operating through a manufacturer or independently, dealers may offer financing, conduct warranty service on the manufacturer's behalf, and enable you to customize your home with options and upgrades—just like a new car.

The largest manufactured home manufacturers operate on a national basis through multiple factory locations, each with a shipping radius of 500 or so miles and supported by a network of both dedicated and independent dealers. In 2002 the top-ten manufactured home companies each shipped an average of more than 15,000 homes, a volume comparable to the largest on-site builders.

The bulk of the industry, however, consists of regional companies operating one or two factories that supply several surrounding states, also within a reasonable shipping distance, through similar dealer networks. As of late 2003 there were 62 companies operating 212 manufacturing plants throughout North America, each building and shipping an average of about 750 homes annually.

Relying on a decentralized management approach, national manufactured home companies operate like their regional counterparts, though perhaps enjoying slightly better economies of scale and standardization given their multiple factories and greater production volume. For the most part, the difference between national and regional companies is all but invisible to home buyers.

The Dealer Dynamic

Though some manufactured and modular home building companies offer *direct sales* from the factory, most prefer (and often insist) that you buy from a local dealer. In addition to providing a local contact point for a manufacturer and/or a factory that might be hundreds of miles away, a dealer is charged with coordinating—and often conducting—the placement and *final assembly* of the house. As a courtesy the dealer may also connect (or manage the connection of) utilities to the home's main *service panel* and schedule the *final inspection* by the local building authority.

In turn, the dealer's participation as a trained and certified representative of the manufactured home company ensures the terms of the warranty against problems or defects related to the home's final placement on your lot. If you hire an outside contractor to coordinate the delivery, *crane placement,* and *final tie-ins* between the home's sections and with its foundation and utilities, the manufacturer will likely void part or perhaps all of its *explicit warranty* on the house.

Manufactured home companies also work directly with local housing developers and builders, as well as with their dealer networks, to supply homes for new subdivisions or mobile home parks that are in turn sold or rented to the public. If you're looking for a building lot or neighborhood, a local manufactured home dealer can provide direction and access to those in the immediate area and/or other markets served by the manufacturer.

Most manufactured home buyers, however, already own or will soon buy a lot (or parcel of land) outside a subdivision or mobile home park setting, typically in a rural area. As long as the land is within the shipping radius of the factory, with safe and passable access to it, the dealer can coordinate the home's delivery and its placement at that location.

Direct sales: Sales made to home owner-buyers directly instead of through a dealer network.

Final assembly: The last bit of work required to complete a manufactured or modular home on the home site; also known as "final tie-ins."

Service panel: A central location to which a utility (e.g., electricity) enters the house and is then distributed throughout the house.

Final inspection: The last scheduled inspection by a third party or independent building department official prior to move-in.

Crane placement: The use of a crane to place or set panels or sections of a home on its foundation.

Final tie-ins: The last bit of work required to complete a manufactured or modular home on the home site; also known as "final assembly."

Explicit warranty: A printed or documented contract to fix legitimate problems within a certain time period.

Local manufactured home dealers are responsible for the shipping, placement, and final assembly of a new home on the owner's lot, but they also offer services outside that scope.

Land-home package: A sale that includes both the house and the parcel of land on which it will be built or placed.

Site improvements: Adding or bringing utility services to and creating a building area (or pad) on a parcel of raw land.

Utility extensions: Bringing utility services (e.g., water) from the main line in the street to the house.

Concrete pad, concrete slab: A slab foundation or other monolithic concrete surface (such as a patio).

Additional Services

In addition to serving as the manufactured home company's local representative, shepherding buyers through the sales process, directing the delivery and placement of their home, and providing warranty work, dealers offer optional services.

For instance, most dealers offer financing, typically through a variety of sources. While few offer in-house financing (when the dealer or manufacturer acts as the lender), most process loan applications through banks, financial institutions, and mortgage lenders gratis, and they will offer free advice as to the various loan programs that suit your circumstances. That said, a dealer's goal is to sell you a home, so it's best to investigate and compare a dealer's financing with that of one or two independent sources.

For a variety of reasons, a mortgage loan for a manufactured home may require slightly different terms and conditions to qualify and gain loan approval. The mortgage amount may also include the land on which the home will be placed, which can actually help secure the loan faster and with better terms because the *land-home package* will be viewed by the lender as more akin to a traditional (nonmobile or permanent) home purchase. Historically, though, landowners lease "pads" to manufactured home owners. See the "Costs and Payment" section later in this chapter for the nuances of financing a manufactured home and chapter 2 for more detail about financing options.

Beyond financing a purchase, or at least the coordination of a loan application, a manufactured home dealer may operate as a building contractor, often as a by-product of his responsibility to place and finish your home's assembly on-site.

For instance, you may choose to employ a dealer's construction services to make necessary *site improvements,* such as excavation, infrastructure (roads, driveways), and *utility extensions* and connections, in preparation for your home's delivery. These improvements, as well as a foundation or *concrete pad* upon which the home will rest, are essential before the home's delivery and placement on your lot.

You might also hire the dealer-contractor to build a garage or other outbuilding not supplied by the manufactured home company (only a few offer factory-built garages), construct a deck or balcony extension, and landscape the property after the home is placed and ready for move-in.

Often a dealer will be able to help you find a parcel of land and may employ or partner with a local real estate agent for that purpose. In some cases a manufactured home dealer will own or have direct access to land, typically in a nearby subdivision or other developed parcel, for purchase with your home—called a land-home package. The dealer (or the manufacturing company), in fact, might be the land's developer or simply an agent or broker for a local builder.

Finally, some dealers offer insurance, **extended warranties,** or other service contracts to sweeten the sales pitch toward providing a turnkey or one-stop home-buying experience.

Your Role

Within the manufactured home-buying process, your role as the eventual owner is no less critical, if slightly different, than with selecting any home-building option.

You are ultimately the boss. It's your responsibility to make the final decisions, work with your builder (or dealer) to establish an agreed-upon set of expectations and needs and then insist that they be met, plus refine and sign the loan and other papers, ask questions and stay informed, hire reputable contractors and pay them on time for the work they've done, and sign off on the final product, assuming it's to your satisfaction.

What's different about manufactured housing is that your decisions up front, specifically about the home's floor plan, **add-ons,** finishes, and options, are final. Once the dealer sends your approved order to the factory to begin the production of your home, you will not be able to make changes.

Depending on your temperament, that fact can be either a relief or a concern. The truth is, change orders occur during the construction of a site-built home primarily because the house is being built before your eyes. You see things during on-site construction that you wouldn't on a house being built in a factory 300 miles away.

To counter any concern about your manufactured or modular home, take your time making decisions regarding the right floor plan, finishes and surfaces, appliances, plumbing fixtures, flooring, and lighting, among other features.

Visit and revisit model homes at the dealer's sales center and, if possible, similar homes built and placed nearby by the same manufacturer/dealer. Take advantage of dealer **showrooms,** or at least samples, of the standard and optional or upgraded finishes you need to choose. Research the products and brands online and/or through other local and independent suppliers. The manufactured home supplier may also provide references to other buyers, who you can call or perhaps visit to get their opinion about the company and the quality of their homes. Take control, make informed decisions, and order your home with confidence.

Extended warranties: Contracts to service problems or defects beyond the standard terms.

Add-ons: Extras, often for an additional price.

Showrooms: Separate locations where a builder, dealer, or supplier may showcase available products, options, and upgrades.

To help mitigate mistakes or misorders, manufacturers insist that both you and the dealer approve the specifications before beginning production of your house. Upon delivery to the local sales center or your home site, the dealer checks the approved order against the house to make sure everything from the floor plan to the finishes is correct. (See the "Inspections and Change Orders" sidebar below.)

Inspections and Change Orders

Though manufacturers and dealers go to great (if appropriate) lengths to make sure you approve your home's specifications before beginning production in the factory, mistakes occasionally occur. Your home will have passed quality checkpoints along the assembly line, but your dealer will inspect your home upon its delivery to the sales center or your home site to make sure it matches up with your order. He'll also look for any defects or damage that might have occurred in transit and walk you through the home to catch any problems.

If he (or you) finds a discrepancy or damage, you can request a change, reorder the home, or agree to live with the mistake. If the problem is nonstructural, such as the wrong carpet or wall covering, the dealer can likely fix it on-site or back at the sales center; structural issues, such as the wrong floor plan or damage to the home's frame or major components (such as windows and doors), will require you to reorder the home and wait through another manufacturing process.

Just like change orders on a site-built home, the cost to make an alteration or fix a problem depends on who is responsible for the mistake or damage. If you decide that the hardwood floor you selected and approved is not what you want once your home arrives, and you can't live with it as is, it'll be on your dime to replace it. By contrast, it is not your financial responsibility to pay for a dealer or manufacturer's mistake.

Rarely, but on occasion, a manufactured or modular home is involved in a traffic accident while being shipped from the factory. Depending on the extent of any damage, the home can be fixed on-site (or at the sales center), but it may need to return to the factory—where it will likely be junked and the order put back in the production queue. Manufacturers typically don't offer damaged homes for resale but rather strip them of reusable parts and finishes for another home.

The Design Process

By the function of assembly-line efficiencies that enable both the low cost and high quality of manufactured homes, the design process is similarly standardized. It's also limited to each manufacturer's proprietary library of available floor plans; the factory is geared only to make homes offered by the manufacturer, not from another company and certainly not from an architect or home designer.

In addition, manufactured homes—by HUD code—are built on a permanent metal chassis that allows the company to install wheels and transport it from the factory to your home site. As such, the dimensions of the house, or each section (also called a "floor") of the house, are limited to federal and state highway restrictions: typically no larger than 16 feet wide and 80 feet long per section.

The fact that a manufactured home has a chassis for a "foundation" also limits design flexibility. Because of weight limitations on the chassis, HUD-code homes are single-story houses, though increasingly designed and built with **volume** (or cathedral) ceilings and ***higher-pitched roofs. Hinged*** roof technology, in which the roof frame is shipped in a low-***slope*** position and then extended to achieve a higher roof pitch on-site, enables more sophisticated manufacturers to create full-height roof attic spaces over the main floor. That extra area can be finished on-site as additional living space, complete with stairs from the main level and site-built or modular

Manufactured and modular homes are built only from the plans offered by each manufacturer to maintain production efficiencies.

Volume: Ceiling heights that are higher than 8 feet.

Higher-pitched roofs: Roof slopes greater than a 4-inch rise for every 12 inches in length.

Hinged (roof): A mechanism that enables higher-pitched roofs on manufactured houses.

Slope: The angle of the roof from its peak or ridge to the eaves.

Hinged roof technology enables modules to be shipped according to highway regulations and allows for pitched roof structures that are appropriate to the style of the house and the surrounding neighborhood.

dormer windows to bring in light. The dimensional and single-story limitations of the HUD code, however, often still result in the long, straight lines and low-sloped roofs that are a telltale sign of a manufactured home.

All those limitations might sound restrictive, but some people find them convenient, not to mention time efficient and affordable. And you can easily adapt the "basic box" using multiple and/or *offset sections,* with decks and balconies, dormers and *entry porticos,* higher-pitched hinged roofs, and garages or other site-built additions that help break up the horizontal lines and *linear massing* of a manufactured home.

Though you will be able to choose only a floor plan offered by the manufacturer, a growing number of companies have become more sophisticated and flexible in adjusting the interior layouts of their manufactured homes by offering optional floor plans within the same *footprint.*

For instance, a double-wide box may be available in dozens of floor plans within the same exterior dimensions, including dual master suites; a home office off the entry; great rooms or large, open living spaces; and larger closets, bedrooms, or bath-

Advances in engineering design and manufacturing technology enable manufactured homes to compete on a level playing field with site-built houses . . . albeit at a much lower per-square-foot cost to build.

rooms. These "options" allow you to customize your home without disrupting the factory-production process. Workers are simply trained to place walls in specified locations on the home's *platform* to accommodate the chosen interior layout.

In addition to selecting from a manufacturer's library of floor plans, you'll have an opportunity to choose many of the exterior and interior finishes and fixtures from a wide range of styles, colors, quality, and performance. Gone are the days when manufactured home builders simply selected the products and offered their homes *as is.* As the rest of the housing industry evolves toward enabling buyers to customize their homes, so does the factory-built housing segment.

With your dealer, or perhaps a design professional hired or contracted by the dealer, you'll walk through a long list of available products and make selections for every room and surface. The manufacturer will offer a list of standard finishes included in the stated price of the home, but you'll also be shown several options and upgrades that expand your choices . . . as well as your budget.

Manufacturers carefully determine the range of options and upgrades to make sure they are mass marketable, are profitable, and will not disrupt the factory-production process. Every item and possible change is prepriced and loaded into a computer program, which automatically and immediately calculates those selected by the home buyer into the sales price of the home. Rarely, though increasingly, manufactured home suppliers are making such information more accessible to buyers via the Internet, enabling consumers to refine their home's design, features, and related costs online.

Manufactured home builders have worked hard to make sure you have a generous choice of products for every room and surface of the house you select. Rarely, if ever, will a manufacturer or dealer allow you to *swap in* a specification that's not on the list, though some may allow you to eliminate a product, such as a kitchen appliance, if you prefer to purchase it separately—assuming the dimensions of the appliance fit in the space provided on the floor plan.

With so many standard and optional choices available these days, however, including luxurious upgrades to some of the finest and highest-performing brands and products available, it's hard to imagine being dissatisfied.

It bears repeating that the decisions you make at this point are final once the home is put into the *production cycle.* Efficiencies up and down the supply chain and the assembly line preclude any changes to the home's list of specifications, from the floor plan to the floor finishes. For that reason, take the time to evaluate your choices thoroughly in terms of priority, performance, and budget before you sign the order for the company to start building your home.

Platform: A horizontal surface upon which to build walls.

As is: In current condition, with no changes.

Swap in: Switch to an alternative, such as a different brand or style of sink or cabinets.

Production cycle: The time between excavation and move-in; the building process.

Concrete pad, concrete slab: A slab foundation or other monolithic concrete surface (such as a patio).

Zoning approval: Authorization to build a certain type of structure in a chosen area.

Building permits: Documentation that confirms approval of construction.

Soil bearing capacity: The ability of the soil to withstand the weight of the finished house.

Skirting: A finish detail around the base of a manufactured (HUD-code) home that conceals the chassis.

Selecting Contractors

Though up to 95 percent of a manufactured home is built in a factory, you'll need to prepare your home site for its delivery, placement, and final assembly. In most cases such work requires one or more contractors who know the nuances of manufactured housing and how to complete the building process once the house arrives at your home site.

At the most basic level, a manufactured home requires a *concrete slab,* or pad, to provide a stable, level surface for its chassis. You'll need to bring various utilities to the site, including electricity, plumbing and/or septic, natural gas, telephone and dial-up Internet service (including DSL), cable television and Internet service, or any combination of these to meet your needs in the home. You must also verify and obtain *zoning approval* and applicable *building permits.* And you'll need to excavate the lot to accommodate one or more tractor trailers and a crane, including *soil bearing capacity.*

Before you move in, the local building authority will require safe access to every door, a *skirting* around the base to hide the chassis, and proper utility hookups before approving the house for occupancy (called a certificate of occupancy, or CO).

Other improvements to the lot are nonessential to a manufactured home, though perhaps important to you, such as a driveway and a garage. You may also choose to dress up your new home once it arrives with decks and balconies, entry porticos, landscaping, and attached or detached structures that were either not available from the manufacturer or more convenient to accomplish on your home site.

Necessary and optional improvements and additions to your manufactured home may require the services of a contractor, perhaps several, to complete the work. Even home

Many jurisdictions and building codes require a skirting or "skirt" around the perimeter of a manufactured home to hide the chassis. You'll likely have to hire a contractor to install the skirting.

owners with the experience and skill to perform these and other jobs themselves may lack the time and energy to do so; a rural location may also present logistical problems that can add costs and delay your home's delivery and your move-in date.

As mentioned, the majority of manufactured home dealers provide construction services that run the gamut of those you'll most likely need or want. As part of the sales contract, they are obliged to coordinate the delivery, placement, and final assembly. The dealer might offer additional services at a discount, or perhaps presented as "free of charge," to entice a sale or as a customer service to ensure your satisfaction and relieve your anxiety.

No doubt a dealer has an attractive level of experience with manufactured homes and would logically know why and how to properly prepare the site for its delivery and placement. Even so, as with the design and product selection process, conduct some research and solicit bids for the same work among other local contractors.

Specifically, contact a few excavation and/or concrete contractors (sometimes one in the same) who specialize in residential work, utility contractors skilled in bringing various services to the property, carpenters, and landscape professionals. All of them should be listed in the local yellow pages by their specialty; consider gathering recommendations from lumberyards, nurseries, and the utility companies, too.

Different theories exist about hiring contractors, but put your faith in their professionalism, experience with similar type of work, financial stability, and reputation as determined by past client references. Set and share your budget with all of them, gather bids (or cost estimates for the work), and compare the numbers with your manufactured home dealer. Red flag and be wary of remarkably low or excessively high bids, but don't let cost be your only, or even your primary, consideration.

Assuming the bids are competitive and based on an identical scope of work, choose the contractor for each task whom you trust will complete the job on your timeline and to your satisfaction. It may well be that your dealer is the best option, but it's worth the effort to find out for sure.

A few things to note about all contractors: Like you, they have a job. They do it every day, just as you do your job, so there's little excitement and emotion tied to it on a daily basis. They also have their own nomenclature and an intimate familiarity with the task, tools, and other trades they rely on to perform their work.

The best contractors understand and respect the fact that you, as the home owner, may have a higher emotional investment—and less familiarity—with the project or task at hand. They are patient in their approach and communication efforts to reassure you.

Piggyback (roof):
A mechanism that enables
higher-pitched roofs on manufactured houses.

**Speculative model
homes:** Completed homes
at a builder's sales center or
subdivision used as a marketing device to sell more
homes.

That being said, don't expect any contractor to get worked up about small details and the unfinished state of the job day to day. Hopefully you'll choose contractors who not only envision the final product and work toward it but also explain that process to you in a language you'll understand. Just be aware that while most contractors may lack the latter skill, they still can be reputable and reliable tradespeople.

The Construction Process

Manufactured homes are built on an assembly line to within 90-plus percent of completion, a process the industry often refers to as "off-site" construction.

Starting with a prewelded chassis, factory workers construct the home's wood-framed platform (or floor) upon which they tilt up and secure prebuilt wall sections, install various floor finishes, windows and doors, plumbing and electrical systems, insulation, and drywall. The entire assembly is set on rails or lifted by crane to enable it to progress from one station to the next along the assembly line.

Meanwhile, the roof frame, complete with a textured ceiling, is built on a separate assembly line and craned into place over the walls and floor. The entire house section then moves to the next station of the assembly line to receive finished roofing, siding, cabinets, appliances, and other fixtures and finishes (see the construction sequence on page 103–8) before it is shipped to your location or to the dealer's sales center on its way to your home site.

Historically, the HUD code and highway transportation safety laws limited the height, and therefore the roof slope, of manufactured and modular homes, resulting in low-pitched rooflines that differentiated them, in a negative way, from site-built houses. Within the last decade, however, hinged and *piggyback* roof trusses allow manufactured and modular homes to achieve steeper roof pitches while still meeting highway regulations. Simply, some or part of the roof lies flat during transit, then is lifted up and connected on-site to create a steeper pitch.

At every stage along the assembly line, and occasionally multiple times, independent and company inspectors make sure the construction follows the HUD code. Quality control staff is also on hand to ensure the structure meets the company's own standards including and beyond health and safety issues. A HUD-code inspector certifies that each finished section (or the completed home) complies with the federal building standard.

In modern facilities, other smaller assembly areas serve the main line. Though each home is built to order (including *speculative model homes* purchased by dealers for marketing and sales purposes), workers prebuild wall sections, construct or assemble

The manufactured home construction sequence.

Step 1: Floor. A wheeled chassis or frame is rolled onto the assembly-line floor, upon which the first-floor platform, including joists and subfloor panels, is built.

Step 2: Exterior walls. In a nearby area of the factory, workers prebuild and insulate the exterior wall sections, which are then craned into place on the floor platform.

Step 3: Exterior walls. Workers use cranes mounted from the roof of the factory to more easily move and place exterior wall sections on the floor platform.

Step 4: Interior walls. Another assembly line builds the interior wall sections according to the plans and specifications of each particular house ordered.

Step 5: Mechanical installation. Once the interior walls are placed on and secured to the platform, workers install plumbing and electrical conduits in the stud cavities.

Step 6: Ceilings. A separate assembly line builds the roof structure, including the ceiling drywall installation, which is then textured to create a finished surface.

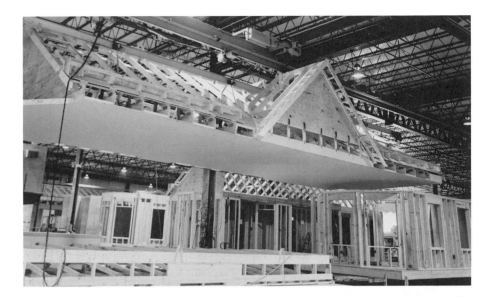

Step 7: Roof installation. The entire roof structure, including the finished ceiling, is then lifted by crane and placed on top of the floor and wall assembly (steps 1–5).

Step 8: Inspection. Prior to the application of the exterior finish (typically siding), third-party inspectors make sure the wall insulation is up to code and installed properly in the wall cavities.

Step 9: Exterior finish. To achieve a high level of energy efficiency, crews wrap the exterior shell of the house with a water-air barrier before attaching the siding—in this case, log veneers that will give the appearance of a rural cabin.

Step 10: Interior finishes. As the exterior shell is completed, workers also apply interior finishes, including cabinets and countertops.

Step 11: Paint. Interior paint is applied with a sprayer, making the job faster and ensuring complete coverage.

Step 12: Inspection. One of several inspections throughout the building process includes a check of the mechanical systems, such as the electrical panel.

Step 13: Final inspection. With the house complete and in the shipping area, an inspector makes one last check of the entire home, noting punch-list items that need to be satisfied before the house is delivered.

Step 14: Shipping. A manufactured home's wheeled chassis comes in handy for shipping homes across long distances, increasingly in sections that will be connected together on the job site as part of the final assembly process.

Step 15: On-site assembly. Sections are craned into place on the foundation and secured to the structure and other sections to create a complete house.

Step 16: Finishing. Finally, the house is skirted (if necessary) and landscaped to give the appearance of a site-built home.

Pneumatic: Driven by compressed air.

cabinets, and precut ceramic tile and other surface finishes in preparation for homes coming down the assembly line. The manufacturer purchases and stocks most of the finishes, including prebuilt windows, doors, siding, and roofing, to keep the line moving quickly.

To supplement the obvious efficiency of the assembly-line process, where home sections move from one station to the next within minutes, manufactured home companies employ ***pneumatic*** nailers and sprayers, various sizes of cranes, and perhaps even robotics and other automated systems to speed the process even more. The largest manufactured home company averages about 112 sections (or floors) per weekday among multiple factories.

Modular versus Manufactured Home Production

Modular homes do not fall under the jurisdiction of the HUD code and are therefore built without a chassis. Instead, modules are constructed and finished in a wood-framed platform only, and they can be stacked to create multistory (and multisection) homes; without a chassis, modular homes more easily enable full basements or crawl-space foundations to expand living space or hide and protect mechanical systems and utilities under the house. The lack of a chassis also means that modular home sections must be shipped in flatbed trucks or trailers (instead of on the integral chassis used for manufactured homes).

Beyond that simple yet critical difference, the production of modular and manufactured homes is nearly identical, including multipoint inspections (albeit to the building code enforced at its final location rather than the federal HUD-code standards)—a fact that allows some of the larger companies to build and sell both types of housing from the same factory.

On-site Assembly

Though a manufactured or modular home is shipped nearly complete from the factory, multisection homes must be connected at the home site, a stage often called "on-site assembly." Nearly 75 percent of manufactured homes purchased and shipped consist of at least two sections.

Upon delivery, sections or modules are placed within a quarter inch or less of each other and connected with preinstalled brackets, bolts, or clamps behind the finished walls and in the roof and floor frame or chassis.

Workers then weave or finish the home's interior and exterior materials to hide the seams between sections, though most sections are connected at either end and along the *roof ridge* (think of a double-wide mobile home), with the vertical seam on the outside masked with a piece of trim or siding. A bit of *tape and texture* to the interior drywall, or the installation of a wall finish such as paneling or wallpaper, hides the seams inside.

To pass inspection and earn a CO, the dealer or utility companies must connect the various and available services to the home's main service panel, build steps and other access to the home, construct balconies or decks, and provide skirting.

Upon the home's final assembly, which can take up to four weeks or so after delivery depending on the home's complexity and finishes, it is ready for final inspection and move-in. At that point, or in the meantime, you can choose to construct an attached or detached garage, add landscaping features, and/or build an entry portico or deck to complete the home to suit your needs.

Costs and Payment

Costs and payment terms depend on the variables of your manufactured home purchase, including the size and features of the finished home, shipping costs, site improvement expenses, and the conditions of your loan.

Historically, and even after amendments to the HUD code defined manufactured homes as "buildings" instead of "vehicles," lenders were reluctant to lend money against a structure that could be moved—regardless of the fact that a scant few manufactured homes built after 1980 are relocated. And manufactured homes were often placed on leased property; while you might own your home, you rented the land, typically in a mobile home park. That scenario precluded lenders from considering manufactured homes as "real" property, and thus the homes carried a higher risk and less value for the bank. As a result, lenders attached higher interest rates and shorter repayment terms for manufactured home loans.

Roof ridge: The top of the roof along a horizontal plane.

Tape and texture: The process for concealing the joints between sheets of gypsum wallboard (drywall) and applying a texture or pattern prior to paint or other wall finish.

Amortized: Spread out over time.

Within the last few years, however, the shift from leased pads at mobile home parks to private property locations and purchased parcels of land, including subdivisions, has brought manufactured homes into the mainstream of mortgage lending. Manufactured homes that are permanently mounted to a foundation on an owner's lot are considered real property, or real estate, and thus present a more attractive risk to mortgage lenders.

In short, do not accept a higher interest rate and/or shorter payment terms simply because you're buying a manufactured home and placing it on a lot you own or are purchasing as part of the overall home sale. Your down payment, interest rate, and terms may be impacted by your credit rating, income and existing debt, and other risk factors or financial conditions, but it should no longer be subject to prejudices against factory-built homes.

Shipping costs are often a concern for manufactured home buyers, especially those planning to locate their new homes in a rural area with perhaps difficult access and a considerable distance from the factory. In fact, manufactured home builders calculate shipping by distance and the number of sections and fold that shipping cost into the final price of your home. If you finance the purchase, the shipping cost is *amortized* in the loan and repaid on a monthly basis.

Even though manufactured homes are a legitimate form of permanent housing, they've been tagged as the one segment of the real estate industry that depreciates, rather than appreciates, in value over time, in large part due to a lingering public perception of poor quality and their placement in less-than-desirable locations or conditions.

Newer versions, especially those in developed subdivisions and neighborhoods, are reversing that fortune and appreciating at a similar pace with site-built homes under similar market conditions and factors. For any type of house, however, the bulk of the property's appreciated value is a function of the land and its location more so than the house or building itself.

Though you will sign a contract to purchase the home upon approval of the specifications prior to its factory production, you will not "close" on the home, or take possession of and financial responsibility for it, until you and your dealer have inspected it and made any necessary or requested changes or repairs. In addition, the local building authority must approve your house for occupancy before you close escrow.

Manufactured Homes: Pros and Cons

Pros

- Faster completion.
- Year-round construction capability.
- Simultaneous on-site improvements and preparation.
- Faster on-site assembly.
- Equal or better structural quality and energy efficiency.
- Steady pricing (not as subject to materials/labor cost fluctuations).
- Less waste (time and materials).
- Significantly lower cost (per square foot and overall).
- Variety of services offered by dealer.

Cons

- Design may be limited by HUD code and highway transportation safety laws.
- Selection of homes from a manufacturer's catalog only.
- Possible zoning restrictions.
- Negative perception among lenders, neighbors, real estate agents, and/or municipal planning departments.
- Single or one-and-a-half-story homes only (not available with full second story).
- No changes allowed once the home is in production.

Warranty and Maintenance

Like any home builder, manufactured home companies offer explicit (or written) and implied (expected) warranties for the homes they build.

Though the precise terms may differ among manufacturers, explicit warranties cover structural workmanship and factory-installed mechanical and utility services, appliances, and other finishes and products. The actual setup or final assembly of the house on your home site is usually covered by the dealer's warranty instead of the manufacturer's. Manufacturer warranties are included in the price of your home, though extended service plans through the company and/or the dealer are also available for an added premium.

Many of the products in your home—most notably the appliances, heating and cooling equipment, roofing and siding, and plumbing fixtures—are often covered by *their* manufacturers as well as the home manufacturer's warranty. In fact, the builder or dealer may refer you to a specific product manufacturer if it's determined that a problem falls under that company's warranty.

Implied warranties are simply an expectation of reliable construction practices, intended performance and use, and adherence to applicable building codes. By most state laws the manufacturer is obliged to deliver a home ready for occupancy.

Given the off-site nature of a manufactured home's construction and the fact that sections are shipped near-complete to your home site, make a diligent effort to get explicit warranty coverage for the home from the factory, along the highway, and on your home site prior to move-in.

With that, understand the terms of coverage, whom to call for service, and what to expect in the way of response time, costs, and your own responsibilities for upkeep. For instance, manufacturer warranties—on the home or any product therein—do not cover wear and tear, accidents, negligence, on-site additions or changes, or unauthorized repairs. Homeowners insurance, which is required with any mortgage loan, covers accidents and acts of nature, while your own diligence covers the rest.

Catalog of Manufactured (HUD-Code) Homes

The companies listed in the following catalog represent the universe of manufactured (or HUD-code) home producers, according to the two national trade associations for the industry and other sources.

With few exceptions these companies operate on a regional basis, using centralized manufacturing operations that ship homes from the factory to local "dealers" or "builders" to sell to home buyers in and for nearby markets. As you use this catalog, then, pay close attention to a company's sales territory more so than its headquarters or mailing address, and be sure to match *where* you plan to build and enjoy your new home with a company's sales realm. Increasingly manufactured homes are being sold as vacation or second homes; if that's your intention, make sure a supplier sells its homes in that location, which may be a different state than your current, primary residence.

Once you find and perhaps narrow your choices of companies to those that serve the intended location of your new home, find out the exact location of the company's nearest sales center to serve you. You'll have to visit the sales center to continue your research and buy your house, which provides opportunities to walk through model homes (a few of which hopefully offer a semblance of what you want and need), learn about options and upgrades (and their costs), and—perhaps most important—gauge the skills and services of the dealer-builder selling you the home.

These days the manufactured home industry's reputation for lack of good housing design is a myth. Sure, the HUD code forbids two-story plans, but for the most part manufactured home producers offer a wide range of square footage, exterior styles, and finish products. Companies that maintain Internet Web sites often provide catalogs of their homes (usually shown as two-dimensional floor plans) based on certain parameters you provide, primarily the size of home you want. Whether online, in a printed catalog, or in a sales/design center, expect to see a range of single-, double-, and triple-wide homes finished inside and out with an impressive variety of choices.

Use the following listings to first narrow your choices among manufactured home producers that sell in the area in which you need a new house, then investigate them on the Web, via e-mail, and by visiting nearby sales/design centers.

During that investigation, confirm that they have the house you want and can deliver it to your location, and ask questions about the financial and construction services provided by the dealer-builder (and perhaps the parent company or manufacturer) so that you know exactly what to expect should you sign a contract for a new manufactured home.

Adrian Homes
Highway 80 East
P.O. Box 266
Adrian, GA 31002
(478) 668–3232; fax: (478) 668–4943
www.adrianhomesmfg.com
Sales territory: FL, GA, NC, SC

Bonna Villa Homes
Division of Chief Industries
111 Grant Street
P.O. Box 127
Aurora, NE 68818
(402) 694–5250; fax: (402) 694–5873
www.bonnavilla.chiefind.com
Sales territory: CO, IA, IL, KS, MN,
MO, MT, ND, NE, SD, WY

Burlington Homes of Maine
620 Maine Street
Oxford, ME 04270
(800) 255–5218; fax: (207) 539–2900
www.burlingtonhomes.com
Sales territory: CT, MA, ME, NH,
NY, RI

**Cappaert Manufactured
Housing**
6200 U.S. Highway 61 South
P.O. Box 820567
Vicksburg, MS 39182
(601) 636–5401; fax: (601) 636–0070
www.cappaert.org
Sales territory: AL, AR, FL, LA, MO,
MS, OK, TN, TX

Cavalier Homes, Inc.
32 Wilson Boulevard, Suite 100
P.O. Box 540
Addison, AL 35540
(256) 747–9800; fax: (256) 747–3044
www.cavhomesinc.com
Sales territory: AL, AR, CO, FL, GA,
IL, KS, KY, LA, MO, MS, NC, NM,
OK, SC, TN, TX, VA

❖ An increasing number of
manufactured home producers
offer houses that replicate the
look of log cabins, primarily to
attract second- or vacation-
home buyers.

Champion Enterprises Inc.
*Including Redman, Moduline,
Summit Crest, Silvercrest, Atlantic,
Titan, Fortune, Commander, Dutch,*

*Gateway, Advantage Homes,
Homes of Merit, and Champion
Homebuilders*
2701 Cambridge Court, Suite 300
Auburn Hills, MI 48326
(248) 340–9090; fax: (248) 340–9345
www.championhomes.net
Sales territory: Nationwide

Chariot Eagle, Inc.
931 Northwest Thirty-seventh
Avenue
Ocala, FL 34475
(352) 629–7007; fax: (352) 629–6920
www.charioteagle.com
Sales territory: Nationwide

Chariot Eagle-West, Inc.
8100 West Buckeye Road
Phoenix, AZ 85043
(623) 936–7545; fax: (623) 936–7012
www.charioteaglewest.com
Sales territory: Nationwide

**Clayton Homes Inc./CMH
Manufacturing**
*Including Clayton Homes, Crest
Homes, Golden West Homes,
Marlette Homes, Oakwood Homes,
and Schult Homes*
P.O. Box 9790
Maryville, TN 37802
(800) 822–0633, (865) 380–3000;
fax: (865) 380–3750
www.clayton.net
Sales territory: Nationwide

**Colony Factory Crafted
Homes**
Division of The Commodore Corp.
P.O. Box 310
Shippenville, PA 16254
(814) 226–9590
www.colony-homes.com
Sales territory: CT, DE, MA, MD,
ME, NH, NJ, NY, PA, RI, VT, WV

Commodore Homes of Indiana
Division of The Commodore Corp.
1902 Century Drive
Goshen, IN 46527
(574) 534–3067; fax: (574) 534–2716
www.commodore-indiana.com
Sales territory: IA, IL, IN, KS, KY, MI,
MO, OH, WI

**Commodore Homes of
Pennsylvania**
Division of The Commodore Corp.
P.O. Box 349
Clarion, PA 16254
(814) 226–9210
www.commodore-pa.com
Sales territory: CT, DE, MA, MD,
ME, NH, NJ, NY, PA, RI, VT, WV

Fairmont Homes
*Including Friendship Homes of
Minnesota*
502 South Oakland
Nappanee, IN 46550
(574) 773–7941; fax: (574) 773–2185
www.fairmonthomes.com
Sales territory: CO, IA, IL, IN, KS,
KY, MD, MN, MO, MT, NC, NE, NH,
NY, OH, PA, SD, VT, WI, WV, WY

The Fall Creek Home, LLC
25603 Borg Road
Elkhart, IN 46514
(866) 274–3113, (574) 523–1444;
fax: (574) 522–4660
www.fallcreekhomes.com
Sales territory: IL, IN, KY, ME, MI,
MN, MO, OH, PA, WI

Fleetwood Homes
Division of Fleetwood Enterprises
Inc.
3125 Myers Street
P.O. Box 7638
Riverside, CA 92513-7638
(909) 351–3500; fax: (909) 351–3697
www.fleetwoodhomes.com
Sales territory: Nationwide

❖ Because they are built in a
factory to a national (HUD)
code, manufactured homes are
generally more energy-efficient
than traditional site-built
houses; an increasing number
of companies and their homes
are certified by the federal
Energy Star program.

**Four Seasons
Manufacturing, Inc.**
P.O. Box 630
Middlebury, IN 46540
(574) 825–9999; fax: (574) 825–2275
www.fourseasonshousing.com

Sales territory: AR, CO, CT, DE, IA, IL, IN, KS, KY, MD, ME, MI, MN, MO, MT, NC, ND, NE, NH, NJ, NY, OH, OK, PA, RI, SD, TN, VA, VT, WI, WV, WY

❖ While making changes to a manufactured home's floor plan is unlikely (as it would impact the factory assembly process and possibly violate the HUD code), some companies offer cosmetic, nonstructural options, such as covered entries and false dormer windows, to add more dimension and interest.

Franklin Homes Inc.
10655 Highway 43
Russellville, AL 35653
(800) 332–4511, (256) 332–4510;
fax: (256) 331–2203
www.franklinhomesusa.com
Sales territory: All states east of Texas

Fuqua Homes
2405 Industrial Drive
P.O. Box 394
Boonville, MO 65233
(800) 777–3896; fax: (660) 882–2480
www.fuquahomes-mo.com
Sales territory: AR, CA, CO, ID, IL, IN, KS, MO, MN, MT, NE, NV, OK, OR, SD, UT, WA, WI, WY

General Manufactured Housing Inc.
P.O. Box 1449
Waycross, GA 31503
(912) 285–5068; fax: (912) 285–1397
www.general-housing.com
Sales territory: AL, FL, GA, LA, NC, SC, TN

Giles Industries, Inc.
405 South Broad Street
New Tazewell, TN 37825
(423) 626–7243; fax: (423) 626–6919
www.gilesindustries.com
Sales territory: AL, AR, GA, IN, KY, MD, MO, MS, NC, NY, OH, SC, TN, VA, WV

Guerdon Enterprises
5556 Federal Way
Boise, ID 83716
(208) 345–5100; fax: (208) 336–9269
www.guerdon.com
Sales territory: CA, CO, ID, NV, OR, UT, WA, WY

Hi-Tech Housing Inc.
19319 County Road 8
Bristol, IN 46507
(800) 837–6449, (574) 848–5593;
fax: (574) 848–5472
www.hi-techhousing.com
Sales territory: Nationwide

Holmes Building Systems, LLC
2863 Plank Road
Robbins, NC 27325
(910) 948–2516; fax: (910) 948–3045
www.hbshome.com
Sales territory: NC, SC, VA

The Homark Co.
100 Third Street
Red Lake Falls, MN 56750
(800) 382–1154, (218) 253–2777;
fax: (218) 253–2116
www.detroiter.com
Sales territory: MI, MN, ND, SD, WI

The Karsten Co., Inc.
P.O. Box 276628
Sacramento, CA 95827
(916) 363–2681; fax: (916) 363–4537
www.thekarstenco.com
Sales territory: Four divisions covering: AK, AR, AZ, CA, CO, ID, KS, LA, MT, NM, NV, OK, OR, TX, UT, WA, WY

❖ In 1995 more than 50 percent of manufactured homes were "single-wide" style; by 2001 that percentage had dropped to 25.3.

KIT Home Builders West, LLC
P.O. Box 250
Caldwell, ID 83606
(208) 454–5000; fax: (208) 454–5029
www.kitwest.com
Sales territory: CA, CO, ID, MT, NV, OR, UT, WA, WY

Lake City Manufactured Housing
10068 Keystone Drive
Lake City, PA 16423
(814) 774–2658; fax: (814) 774–9192
www.lakecityhomes.com
Sales territory: NY, OH, PA

❖ The average age of a manufactured home owner is 52.6, though 46 percent of owners are younger than 50.

Liberty Homes
1001 Eisenhower Drive North
Goshen, IN 46540
(800) 733–0431, (574) 533–0431
www.libertyhomes.com
Sales territory: IL, IN, KY, MI, MO, OH

Magnolia Homes
P.O. Box 657
Gering, NE 69341
(308) 436–3131; fax: (308) 436–1965
www.magnoliahomes.biz
Sales territory: CO, KS, NE, SD, UT, WY

Manufactured Housing Enterprises Inc.
09302 State Road 6
Bryan, OH 43506
(800) 821–0220, ext. 200, (419) 636–4511; fax: (419) 636–4322
www.mheinc.com
Sales territory: CO, CT, IA, IL, KY, MI, MO, NJ, NY, OH, PA, TN, VA, WI, WV

❖ About one-third of manufactured homes are placed in finished communities or subdivisions, while 67 percent are located on private property.

Nashua Homes of Idaho
5200 South Federal Way
Boise, ID 83716
(208) 345–0222; fax: (208) 345–1144
www.nashuahomesofidaho.com
Sales territory: AK, AZ, CA, CO, ID, MT, NV, OR, UT, WA, WY

Nobility Homes
3741 Southwest Seventh Street
P.O. Box 1659
Ocala, FL 34474
(352) 732–5157; fax: (352) 622–6766
www.nobilityhomes.com
Sales territory: FL

Oak Creek Manufactured Homes
Division of American Homestar
Corp.
2450 South Shore Boulevard,
Suite 300
League City, TX 77573
(281) 334–9700; fax: (281) 334–9737
www.oakcreekhomes.com/manu
factured
Sales territory: CO, LA, NM, OK, TX

Palm Harbor Homes, Inc.
*Including Discovery Custom Homes
(modular)*
15303 Dallas Parkway, Suite 800
Addison, TX 75001–4600
(972) 991–2422; fax: (972) 764–9014
www.palmharbor.com
Sales territory: AL, AZ, CA, CO, FL,
GA, ID, IL, IN, KY, LA, MI, NC, NM,
NV, OH, OK, OR, SC, TN, TX, VA, WA

❖ By 2000, 22 million people
(or 8 percent of the U.S. popu-
lation) lived full-time in manufactured homes.

Patriot Homes Inc.
307 South Main Street, Suite 200
Elkhart, IN 46516
(574) 524–8600; fax: (574) 524–8640
www.patriothomes.com
Sales territory: AL, AR, CO, DE, FL,
GA, IA, IL, IN, KS, KY, LA, ME, MI,
MN, MO, MT, NE, NM, NY, OH, OK,
PA, SD, TN, TX, VA, VT, WI, WV, WY

❖ More than seventy-five
manufactured home produc-
tion manufacturers are certified to build homes that
qualify under the federal
Energy Star program.

Pine Grove Manufactured Homes, Inc.
2 Pleasant Valley Road
P.O. Box 128
Pine Grove, PA 17963
(570) 345–2811; fax: (570) 345–2676
www.pinegrovehomes.com
Sales territory: CT, DC, DE, MA,
MD, ME, NH, NJ, NY, OH, PA, RI,
VA, VT, WV

R-Anell Housing Group LLC
3549 North Highway 16
P.O. Box 428
Denver, NC 28037
(704) 483–5511; fax: (704) 483–5674
www.r-anell.com
Sales territory: AL, FL, GA, NC, SC,
TN, VA, WV

Ritz-Craft Corp.
15 Industrial Park Road
P.O. Box 70
Mifflinburg, PA 17844
(800) 326–9836; fax: (570) 966–9248
www.ritz–craft.com
Sales territory: CT, DE, GA, IA, IL,
IN, KY, MA, MD, ME, MI, MO, NC,
NH, NJ, NY, OH, PA, RI, SC, TN, UT,
VA, WV, WI

SEhomes, Inc.
*Including Energy Homes, Southern
Homes, Energy of Texas, and
Southern Estates*
P.O. Box 390
Addison, AL 35540
(256) 747–8589; fax: (256) 747–7586
www.sehomes.com
Sales territory: Southern United
States, including Texas

Shamrock Homes
1201 West Markley Road
Plymouth, IN 46563
(574) 935–5111; fax: (574) 935–4015
www.shamrock-homes.com
Sales territory: IL, IN, MA, MI, MO,
NJ, NY, OH, PA, RI, WI

Skyline Corp.
2520 By-Pass Road
P.O. Box 743
Elkhart, IN 46514
(800) 348–7469, (574) 294–6521;
fax: (574) 293–7574
www.skylinecorp.com
Sales territory: CA, FL, IN, KS, LA,
OH, OR, PA, TX, VT, WI

Sunshine Homes
P.O. Box 507
Red Bay, AL 35582
(256) 356–4427
www.sunshinehomes-inc.com
Sales territory: AL, AR, FL, GA, IA,
KS, KY, LA, MO, MS, NC, OK, SC,
TN, TX

❖ The top-ten states for HUD-
code homes (number of homes
shipped) are: Florida (with
15,582 homes in 2004), Texas,
California, North Carolina,
Tennessee, Kentucky, Louisiana,
Arizona, Georgia, and
Pennsylvania; together the top
ten account for 52.7 percent of
all HUD-code home shipments.

Valley Quality Homes
1830 South First Street
Yakima, WA 98903
(509) 453–8937; fax: (509) 575–7702
www.valleyqualityhomes.com
Sales territory: ID, OR, WA

Wick Building Systems Inc.
2301 East Fourth Street
Marshfield, WI 54449-0530
(715) 387–2551; fax: (715) 384–5346
www.wickmarshfield.com
Sales territory: IA, IL, MI, MN, MO,
MT, ND, NE, SD, WI, WY

Manufactured (HUD-Code) Homes by State and Sales Territory

ALABAMA

Cavalier Homes Inc. (serving AL, AR, CO, FL, GA, IL, KS, KY, LA, MO, MS, NC, NM, OK, SC, TN, TX, VA)

Franklin Homes Inc. (serving all states east of Texas)

SEhomes, Inc. *(includes Energy Homes, Southern Homes, Energy of Texas, and Southern Estates;* serving southern United States, including Texas)

Sunshine Homes (serving AL, AR, FL, GA, IA, KS, KY, LA, MO, MS, NC, OK, SC, TN, TX)

ARIZONA

Chariot Eagle-West, Inc. (nationwide)

CALIFORNIA

Fleetwood Homes (nationwide)

The Karsten Co., Inc. (four divisions serving AK, AR, AZ, CA, CO, ID, KS, LA, MT, NM, NV, OK, OR, TX, UT, WA, WY)

FLORIDA

Chariot Eagle, Inc. (nationwide)

Nobility Homes (serving FL)

GEORGIA

Adrian Homes (serving FL, GA, NC, SC)

General Manufactured Housing Inc. (serving AL, FL, GA, LA, NC, SC, TN)

IDAHO

Guerdon Enterprises (serving CA, CO, ID, OR, NV, UT, WA, WY)

KIT Home Builders West, LLC (serving CA, CO, ID, MT, NV, OR, UT, WA, WY)

Nashua Homes of Idaho (serving AK, AZ, CA, CO, ID, MT, NV, OR, UT, WA, WY)

INDIANA

Commodore Homes of Indiana (serving IA, IL, IN, KS, KY, MI, MO, OH, WI)

Fairmont Homes (serving CO, IA, IL, IN, KS, KY, MD, MN, MO, MT, NC, NE, NH, NY, OH, PA, SD, VT, WI, WV, WY)

The Fall Creek Home, LLC (serving IL, IN, KY, ME, MI, MN, MO, OH, PA, WI)

Four Seasons Manufacturing, Inc. (serving AR, CO, CT, DE, IA, IL, IN, KS, KY, MD, ME, MI, MN, MO, MT, NC, ND, NE, NH, NJ, NY, OH, OK, PA, RI, SD, TN, VA, VT, WI, WV, WY)

Hi-Tech Housing, Inc. (nationwide)

Liberty Homes (serving IL, IN, KY, MI, MO, OH)

Patriot Homes, Inc. (serving AL, AR, CO, DE, FL, GA, IA, IL, IN, KS, KY, LA, ME, MI, MN, MO, MT, NE, NM, NY, OH, OK, PA, SD, TN, TX, VA, VT, WI, WV, WY)

Shamrock Homes (serving IL, IN, MA, MI, MO, NJ, NY, OH, PA, RI, WI)

Skyline Corp. (serving CA, FL, IN, KS, LA, OH, OR, PA, TX, VT, WI)

MAINE

Burlington Homes of Maine (serving CT, MA, ME, NH, NY, RI)

MICHIGAN

Champion Enterprises Inc. (nationwide)

MINNESOTA

The Homark Co. (serving MI, MN, ND, SD, WI)

MISSISSIPPI

Cappaert Manufactured Housing (serving AL, AR, FL, LA, MO, MS, OK, TN, TX)

MISSOURI

Fuqua Homes (serving AR, CA, CO, ID, IL, IN, KS, MN, MO, MT, NE, NV, OK, OR, SD, UT, WA, WI, WY)

NEBRASKA

Bonna Villa Homes (serving CO, IA, IL, KS, MN, MO, MT, ND, NE, SD, WY)

NORTH CAROLINA

Holmes Building Systems, LLC (serving NC, SC, VA)

Magnolia Homes (serving CO, KS, NE, SD, UT, WY)

R-Anell Housing Group, LLC (serving AL, FL, GA, NC, SC, TN, VA, WV)

OHIO

Manufactured Housing Enterprises, Inc. (serving CO, CT, IA, IL, KY, MI, MO, NJ, NY, OH, PA, TN, VA, WI, WV)

PENNSYLVANIA

Colony Factory Crafted Homes (serving CT, DE, MA, MD, ME, NH, NJ, NY, PA, RI, VT, WV)

Lake City Manufactured Housing (serving NY, OH, PA)

Pine Grove Manufactured Homes, Inc. (serving CT, DC, DE, MA, MD, ME, NH, NJ, NY, OH, PA, RI, VA, VT, WV)

Ritz-Craft Corp. (serving CT, DE, GA, IA, IL, IN, KY, MA, MD, ME, MI, MO, NC, NH, NJ, NY, OH, PA, RI, SC, TN, UT, VA, WV, WI)

TENNESSEE

Clayton Homes Inc./CMH Manufacturing (nationwide)

TEXAS

Oak Creek Manufactured Homes (division of American Homestar Corp.; serving CO, NM, LA, OK, TX)

Palm Harbor Homes, Inc. (serving AL, AZ, CA, CO, FL, GA, ID, IL, IN, KY, LA, MI, NC, NM, NV, OH, OK, OR, SC, TN, TX, VA, WA)

WASHINGTON

Valley Quality Homes (serving ID, OR, WA)

WISCONSIN

Wick Building Systems, Inc. (serving IA, IL, MI, MN, MO, MT, NE, ND, SD, WI, WY)

Catalog of Modular Homes

The modular home companies listed here are the leaders in the industry based on the number of homes they produce annually, among other factors including industry involvement, variety of plans, and geographic distribution. They have been culled from the Building Systems Councils of the National Association of Home Builders (NAHB), among other sources.

Modular homes are becoming a popular option among professional builders seeking to speed on-site construction. Like manufactured (HUD-code) homes, modulars are built in a factory; in fact, an increasing number of manufactured home producers also produce modular homes in the same building.

Unlike manufactured homes, however, modulars are subject to the prevailing building codes in the area in which the home will eventually be located, similar to a traditional site-built home, instead of a federal building code. The primary advantages to modular construction, then, are that most of it occurs in a factory (or "off-site"), thereby reducing the time and labor required to build and finish a home on-site, and that it usually offers a wider range of designs than a manufactured home, including two-story houses.

Modular homes are sold mostly to professional builders. Often a builder will act as a local sales representative for a modular home company that has production operations within a radius of a few hundred miles. Like the manufactured home dealer-builder, she presents the company's houses to prospective buyers, negotiates and closes the sale on the company's behalf, and manages the delivery and final assembly of the house on the buyer's lot.

For people interested in buying a modular house, the companies listed in this catalog can provide you with an overview of their homes and construction methods and materials and direct you to a local representative for specific details and contract negotiations. Unless you have the skills and equipment to complete the home's assembly on your own (an especially tricky venture for multistory modular homes), few (if any) of these companies will sell a house directly to you; rather, to ensure the home's proper completion and building code compliance, they require buyers to work with local builder representatives or independent local contractors.

That said, use the catalog to find modular home producers that sell homes in the area in which you want to build your new house, investigate them online and through sales literature, and narrow your choices to those that can meet your specifications for square footage and style of house, as well as construction services, before contacting a local builder representative of the company.

All American Homes, LLC
309 South Thirteenth Street
Decatur, IN 46733
(260) 724–8044; fax: (260) 724–8094
www.allamericanhomes.com
Sales territory: All states *except*
along West Coast, AZ, ID, NV, and
North Atlantic coast/New England
(see online map)

Alouette Homes
aka Home Team Corp.
319 Principale Ouest
Sainte Anne de la Rochelle, PQ
J0E 2B0 Canada
(450) 539–3100 (Canada), (603)
228–2004 (USA); fax: (450)
539–0335
www.alouettehomes.com
Sales territory: Eastern Canada and
New England

Apex Homes, Inc.
Including Alpine Modular Homes
247 U.S. Highway 522 North
Middleburg, PA 17842
(800) 326–9524, (570) 837–2333;
fax: (570) 837–2346
www.apexhomesinc.com
Sales territory: CT, DE, MA, MD,
ME, MI, NC, NH, NJ, NY, OH, PA, RI,
SC, VA, VT, WV

Avis America, Inc.
Henry Street
P.O. Box 420
Avis, PA 17721
(800) 233–3052, (570) 753–3700;
fax: (570) 753–3291
www.avisamerica.com
Sales territory: CT, DE, GA, MA,
MD, ME, KY, NC, NH, NJ, NY, OH,
PA, RI, SC, TN, VA, VT, WV

Benchmark Industries
630 Hay Avenue
Brookville, OH 45309
(937) 833–4091; fax: (937) 833–5268
www.benchmark-homes.com
Sales territory: KY, MI, OH

Beracah Homes
9590 Nanticoke Business Park Drive
Greenwood, DE 19950
(302) 349–4561; fax: (302) 349–5837
www.beracahhomes.com
Sales territory: DE, MD, VA

Capsys Corp.
155 Third Street
Brooklyn, NY 11231
(718) 403–0050; fax: (718) 643–4820
www.capsyscorp.com
Sales territory: Nationwide

Cardinal Homes, Inc.
525 Barnesville Highway (U.S.
Highway 15)
P.O. Box 10
Wylliesburg, VA 23976
(434) 735–8111; fax: (434) 735–8824
www.cardinalhomes.com
Sales territory: SC, VA, WV

Carolina Building Solutions
220 Ryan Patrick Drive
Salisbury, NC 28147
(800) 749–5203, (704) 633–5200;
fax: (704) 633–5282
www.cbsmods.com
Sales territory: GA, NC, SC, TN,
VA, WV

Cavco Industries, LLC
1001 North Central Avenue, Eighth
Floor
Phoenix, AZ 85004
(602) 256–6263; fax: (602) 256–6189
www.cavco.com
Sales territory: AZ, CA, CO, NM,
NV, UT

❖ Unlike manufactured (or
HUD-code) manufacturers, the
vast majority of modular home
manufacturers sell only to
builders, not directly to home
owners.

Celtic Homes
12345–121 Street
Edmonton, AB T5L 4Y7 Canada
(877) 488–1307, (780) 488–1307;
fax: (780) 488–1316
www.celtichomes.ab.ca
Sales territory: Western Canada
and United States

Champion Enterprises Inc.
*Including Redman, Moduline,
Summit Crest, Silver Crest, Atlantic,
Titan, Fortune, Commander, Dutch,
Gateway, Advantage Homes,
Homes of Merit, and Champion
Homebuilders*
2701 Cambridge Court, Suite 300
Auburn Hills, MI 48326
(248) 340–9090; fax: (248) 340–9345
www.championhomes.net
Sales territory: Nationwide

Chariot Eagle, Inc.
931 Northwest Thirty-seventh
Avenue
Ocala, FL 34475
(352) 629–7007; fax: (352) 629–6920
www.charioteagle.com
Sales territory: Nationwide

Chariot Eagle-West, Inc.
8100 West Buckeye Road
Phoenix, AZ 85043
(623) 936–7545; fax: (623) 936–7012
www.charioteaglewest.com
Sales territory: Nationwide

Chelsea Modular Homes, Inc.
Route 9 West
P.O. Box 1108
Marlboro, NY 12542
(845) 236–3311; fax: (845) 236–4881
www.chelseamodular.com
Sales territory: CT, MA, ME, NH, NJ,
NY, PA, RI, VT

**Clayton Homes Inc./CMH
Manufacturing**
*Including Clayton Homes, Crest
Homes, Golden West Homes,
Marlette Homes, Oakwood Homes,
and Schult Homes*
P.O. Box 9790
Maryville, TN 37802
(800) 822–0633, (865) 380–3000;
fax: (865) 380–3750
www.clayton.net
Sales territory: Nationwide

Commodore Homes of Indiana
Division of The Commodore Corp.
1902 Century Drive
Goshen, IN 46527
(574) 534–3067; fax: (574) 534–2716
www.commodore-indiana.com
Sales territory: IA, IL, IN, KS, KY, MI,
MO, OH, WI

**Commodore Homes of
Pennsylvania**
Division of The Commodore Corp.
P.O. Box 349
Clarion, PA 16254
(814) 226–9210
www.commodore-pa.com
Sales territory: CT, DE, MA, ME,
MD, NH, NJ, NY, PA, RI, VT, WV

Contempri Industries, Inc.
1000 West Water Street
P.O. Box 69
Pinckneyville, IL 62274
(618) 357–5361; fax: (618) 357–6629
www.contemprihomes.com
Sales territory: IA, IL, KY, LA, MO,
MN, TN, WI

❖ Most modular home manu-
facturers encourage visitors to
go to their Web sites to fill out
a "request for information"
form to determine where they
are located and their level of
interest in buying a new home.
This is also a place to submit
comments and questions. For
many, the form replaces a standard e-mail submission or
address.

Crest Homes
Division of Schult Homes Corp.
30 Industrial Park
Milton, PA 17847
(570) 742–8521; fax: (570) 742–3842
www.cresthomes.com
Sales territory: CE, DC, DE, GA, IA,
IL, IN, KY, MA, MD, ME, MI, MO,
NC, NH, NJ, NY, OH, PA, RI, SC, TN,
VA, VT, WV, WI

Crestline Homes
5880 Crestline Road
Laurinburg, NC 28352
(800) 366–2981, (910) 276–0195;

fax: (910) 276–4794
www.crestlinehomes.com
Sales territory: GA, NC, SC, VA, TN

Custom Touch Homes, Inc.
P.O. Box 530
Madison, SD 57042
(605) 256–9485; fax: (605) 256–9883
www.customtouchhomes.com
Sales territory: CO, IA, KS, MN, MT,
ND, NE, SD, WY

Customized Structures, Inc.
272 River Road
P.O. Box 884
Claremont, NH 03743
(800) 523–2033; fax: (603) 542–5650
www.customizedstructures.com
Sales territory: CT, MA, ME, NH, NY,
RI, VT

**Deluxe Homes of
Pennsylvania, Inc.**
499 West Third Street
Berwick, PA 18603
(800) 843–7372, (570) 752–5914;
fax: (570) 752–1525
www.deluxehomes.com
Sales territory: CT, DE, MA, MD,
NH, NJ, NY, PA, RI, VA, VT, WV, and
the Caribbean

Design Homes, LLC
11 Edwards Drive
Bloomsburg, PA 17815
(800) 242–5377, (570) 757–1001;
fax: (570) 757–1013
www.designhomesllc.com
Sales territory: CT, DE, MD, ME, MI,
NH, NJ, NY, OH, PA, RI, VA, VT, WV

Discovery Custom Homes
*See Palm Harbor Homes, Inc.,
below.*

Dynamic Homes, LLC
525 Roosevelt Avenue
Detroit Lakes, MN 56502
(218) 847–2611; fax: (218) 847–2617
www.dynamichomes.com
Sales territory: IA, ND, NE, MN,
SD, WI

Epoch Corp.
Route 106
P.O. Box 234
Pembroke, NH 03275
(877) 463–7624, (603) 225–3907;

fax: (603) 225–8329
www.epochhomes.com
Sales territory: CT, MA, ME, NH, NY,
RI, VT

Excel Homes
2595 Interstate Drive, Suite 101
Harrisburg, PA 17100
(717) 651–1500; fax: (717) 651–7742
www.excelhomes.com
Sales territory: CT, DE, GA, KY, MA,
MD, MI, NC, NH, NJ, NY, OH, PA, RI,
SC, TN, VA, VT, WV

Fleetwood Homes
Division of Fleetwood Enterprises
Inc.
3125 Myers Street
P.O. Box 7638
Riverside, CA 92513–7638
(909) 351–3500; fax: (909) 351–3697
www.fleetwoodhomes.com
Sales territory: Nationwide

❖ Design flexibility allows
modulars to be used for a
range of housing types and
styles, including multifamily
homes and commercial buildings.

Foremost Industries, Inc.
2375 Buchanan Trail West
Greencastle, PA 17225
(717) 597–7166; fax: (717) 597–5579
www.foremosthomes.com
Sales territory: MD, PA, VA, WV

Four Seasons Housing
P.O. Box 630
Middlebury, IN 46540
(800) 547–5011, (574) 825–9999;
fax: (574) 825–2275
www.fourseasonshousing.com
Sales territory: AR, CO, CT, DE, IA,
IL, IN, KS, KY, MD, ME, MI, MN,
MO, MT, NC, NE, NH, NJ, NY, OH,
OK, PA, RI, SD, TN, VA, VT, WI,
WV, WY

Fuqua Homes
2405 Industrial Drive
P.O. Box 394
Boonville, MO 65233
(800) 777–3896; fax: (660) 882–2480
www.fuquahomes-mo.com
Sales territory: AR, CA, CO, ID, IL,

IN, KS, MN, MO, MT, NE, NV, OK, OR, SD, UT, WA, WI, WY

Future Home Technology, Inc.
33 Ralph Street
P.O. Box 4255
Port Jervis, NY 12771
(800) 342–8650, (845) 856–9033;
fax: (845) 858–2488
www.futurehometechnology.com
Sales territory: CT, DE, MA, MD, ME, NH, NJ, NY, PA, RI, VT

General Housing Corp.
4650 East Wilder Road
Bay City, MI 48706
(800) 351–3664; fax: (989) 684–2914
www.genhouse.com
Sales territory: MI

Genesis Homes
2701 Cambridge Court, Suite 220
Auburn Hills, MI 48326
(248) 276–1459; fax: (248) 276–1498
www.genesishomes.com
Sales territory: AR, AZ, CA, CO, CT, DE, FL, GA, IA, IL, IN, KS, KY, LA, MD, MI, MN, MO, MS, NC, ND, NE, NH, NJ, NM, NV, OH, OK, PA, RI, SC, SD, TN, TX, UT, VA, VT, WI, WV, WY

Grafton Homes
U.S. Highway 119 South
Grafton, WV 26354
(866) BUILDGH, (304) 265–5353;
fax: (304) 265–5355
www.buildgh.com
Sales territory: MD, PA, VA, WV

Guerdon Enterprises
5556 Federal Way
Boise, ID 83716
(208) 345–5100; fax: (208) 336–9269
www.guerdon.com
Sales territory: CA, CO, ID, NV, OR, UT, WA, WY

Guildcrest Homes
20 Mill Street
Morewood, ON K0A 2R0 Canada
(800) 249–1432, (613) 448–2349;
fax: (613) 448–3464
www.guildcrest.com
Sales territory: Ontario, Quebec, CT, NH, NY, VT

HandCrafted Homes, LLC
101 Eastern Minerals Road
Henderson, NC 27536
(877) 424–4321, (252) 436–0001;
fax: (252) 430–6662
www.handcraftedhomes.com
Sales territory: GA, NC, SC, TN, VA

❖ Use the Web to investigate modular home manufacturers and the dealer-builders in your area; most manufacturer Web sites include the company's full range of floor plans and homes and often a gallery of factory and/or on-site construction photos for your reference.

Haven Homes, Inc.
554 Eagle Valley Road
P.O. Box 178
Beech Creek, PA 16822
(570) 962–2111; fax: (570) 962–3181
www.havenhomes.com
Sales territory: CT, DE, FL, GA, MA, MD, NC, NH, NJ, NY, OH, PA, RI, SC, VA, VT, WV

Heckaman Homes
2676 East Market Street
Nappanee, IN 46550
(574) 773–4167; fax: (574) 773–2546
www.heckamanhomes.com
Sales territory: IL, IN, MI, OH

Heritage Homes of Nebraska
1320 East Seventh (East Highway 35)
Box 37
Wayne, NE 68787
(800) 759–2782; fax: (402) 375–4770
www.heritagehomesofne.com
Sales territory: CO, IA, KS, MN, MO, NE, SD, WY

Hi-Tech Housing Inc.
19319 County Road 8
Bristol, IN 46507
(800) 837–6449, (574) 848–5593;
fax: (574) 848–5472
www.hi-techhousing.com
Sales territory: Nationwide

Holly Park
See Pleasant St. Homes, below.

Homes by IBS
Division of Indiana Building Systems, LLC
51700 Lovejoy Drive
Middlebury, IN 46540
(574) 825–4206; fax: (574) 825–6106
www.homesbyibs.com
Sales territory: IA, IL, IN, KY, MI, MN, MO, OH, WI, WV

Homes by Keystone, Inc.
13338 Midvale Road
Box 69
Waynesboro, PA 17268
(800) 890–7926, (717) 762–1104;
fax: (717) 762–1106
www.homesbykeystone.com
Sales territory: MD, PA, VA, WV

Horton Homes
101 Industrial Boulevard
P.O. Drawer 4410
Eatonton, GA 31024
(800) 657–4000, (706) 485–8506;
fax: (706) 485–4446
www.hortonhomes.com
Sales territory: FL, GA, KY, NC, SC, TN, VA, WV

Huntington Homes, Inc.
3444 Fassett Road
P.O. Box 99
East Montpelier, VT 05651
(802) 479–3625; fax: (802) 479–0575
www.huntingtonhomesvt.com
Sales territory: New England

Integrity Building Systems
2435 Housels Run Road
Milton, PA 17847
(570) 522–3600; fax: (570) 522–0074
www.integritybuild.com
Sales territory: CT, DE, MA, MD,
NH, NJ, NY, PA, RI, VA, WV

**Irontown Housing
Company, Inc.**
2202 South Mountain Vista Lane
Provo, UT 84606
(877) 849–1215, (801) 375–7486;
fax: (801) 375–8399
www.irontownhomes.com
Sales territory: AZ, CA, CO, ID, MT,
NM, OR, UT, WA, WY

❖ Take advantage of online
directories to find an author-
ized builder in your area for
the modular home you want.

Jacobsen Homes
600 Packard Court
P.O. Box 368
Safety Harbor, FL 34695
(727) 726–1138; fax (727) 726–7019
www.jachomes.com
Sales territory: FL

Keiser Industries
56 Mechanic Falls Road
P.O. Box 56
Oxford, ME 04270
(888) 333–1748; fax: (207) 539–4446
www.keisermaine.com
Sales territory: CT, MA, ME, NH

Manorwood Homes
Division of The Commodore Corp.
6 Pleasant Valley Road (Route 443
East)
P.O. Box 169
Pine Grove, PA 17963
(570) 345–0387; fax: (570) 345–6003
www.manorwood.com
Sales territory: CT, DE, GA, MA,
MD, ME, NC, NH, NJ, NY, PA, RI, SC,
TN, VA, VT, WV

**Manufactured Housing
Enterprises Inc.**
09302 State Road 6
Bryan, OH 43506
(800) 821–0220, ext. 200, (419)
636–4511; fax: (419) 636–4322
www.mheinc.com
Sales territory: CO, CT, IA, IL, KY,
MI, MO, NJ, NY, OH, PA, TN, VA,
WI, WV

**Maximum Advantage Building
Systems**
*Formerly Mid-Atlantic Building
Systems*
967 NC Highway 211 East
Candor, NC 27229
(910) 974–9000; (910) 974–9006
www.mabsbuilt.com
Sales territory: GA, NC, SC, TN, VA

Mod-U-Kraft Homes LLC
P.O. Box 573
Rocky Mount, VA 24151
(888) MOD–KRAFT, (540) 483–0291;
fax: (540) 483–2228
www.mod-u-kraft.com
Sales territory: DE, GA, KY, MD, NC,
OH, PA, SC, TN, VA, WV

Modular Structures of PA
1910 North Old Trail
Selinsgrove, PA 17870
(888) 674–6372, (570) 743–2012;
fax: (570) 743–2018
www.msiofpa.com
Sales territory: CT, MD, MI, NC, NJ,
NY, OH, PA, VA, WV

Muncy Homes, Inc.
*Including Superior Builders and
Premier Builders*
1567 PA Route 442
Muncy, PA 17756
(570) 546–5444; fax: (570) 546–5903
www.muncyhomesinc.com
Sales territory: CT, DE, MA, MD,
ME, NH, NJ, NY, PA, RI, VA, VT, WV

Nationwide Homes, Inc.
Division of Palm Harbor Homes
1100 Rives Road
P.O. Box 5511
Martinsville, VA 24115
(800) 216–7001; fax: (276) 666–2537
www.nationwide-homes.com
Sales territory: NC, VA

New England Homes, Inc.
270 Ocean Road
Greenland, NH 03840
(800) 800–8831; fax: (603) 431–8540
www.newenglandhomes.com
Sales territory: New England

❖ An increasing number of
builders, including national
brands that operate in several
markets throughout the country, are turning to modulars to
achieve greater quality, reduce
labor and materials costs, and
hasten cycle time (the amount
of time it takes to complete a
house).

New Era Building Systems
451 Southern Avenue
P.O. Box 269
Strattanville, PA 16258
(877) 678–5581, (814) 764–5581;
fax: (814) 764–5658
www.new-era-homes.com
Sales territory: CT, DE, IL, IN, MA,
MD, ME, MI, NC, NH, NJ, NY, OH,
PA, RI, SC, VA, VT, WI, WV

North Star Modular Homes
300 Legion Field Road
Marshall, MN 56258
P.O. Box 1038
Tracy, MN 56175
(507) 537–0775; fax: (507) 537–0877
http://yourmodular.com
Sales territory: MN, ND, SD, WI, WY

Oak Creek Modular Homes
Division of American Homestar
Corp.
2450 South Shore Boulevard,
Suite 300
League City, TX 77573
(281) 334–9700; fax: (281) 334–9737
www.oakcreekhomes.com/modular
Sales territory: CO, LA, NM, OK, TX

Octa-Structure International, Inc.
2516 West Twenty-third Street
Panama City, FL 32405
(800) 448–4062; fax: (850) 763–6928
www.octastructure.com
Sales territory: Nationwide

Oxford Homes, Inc.
7 Oxford Homes Lane
P.O. Box 679
Oxford, ME 04270-0679
(800) 341–0436, (207) 539–4412;
fax: (207) 539–4259
www.oxfordhomesinc.com
Sales territory: ME, NH, VT

Palm Harbor Homes, Inc.
Including Discovery Custom Homes (modular)
15303 Dallas Parkway, Suite 800
Addison, TX 75001-4600
(972) 991–2422; fax: (972) 764–9014
www.palmharbor.com
Sales territory: AL, AZ, CA, CO, FL, GA, ID, IL IN, KY, LA, MI, NC, NM, NV, OH, OK, OR, SC, TN, TX, VA, WA

Parti, LLC
740 Winterville Road
Athens, GA 30605
(706) 613–1986; fax: (706) 613-2002
www.parti.us
Sales territory: AL, FL, GA, NC, SC, TN

Patriot Homes Inc.
307 South Main Street, Suite 200
Elkhart, IN 46516
(574) 524–8600; fax: (574) 524–8640
www.patriothomes.com
Sales territory: AL, AR, CO, DE, FL, GA, IA, IL IN, KS, KY, LA, ME, MI, MN, MO, MT, NE, NM, NY, OH, OK, PA, SD, TN, TX, VA, VT, WI, WV, WY

Penn Lyon Homes Corp.
101 Airport Road
P.O. Box 27
Selinsgrove, PA 17870
(800) 788–4754; fax: (570) 374–8593
www.pennlyon.com
Sales territory: CT, DE, MA, MD, NH, NJ, NY, PA, RI, VA, VT

Pennwest Homes
Division of The Commodore Corp.
4 Pennwest Way (State Road 38)
Emlenton, PA 16373
(724) 867–0047; fax: (724) 867–0788
www.pennwesthomes.com
Sales territory: CT, DE, MA, MD, ME, NH, NJ, NY, PA, RI, VT, WV

❖ Unlike manufactured (or HUD-code) homes, modular homes can be built with a full second story.

Pinnacle Building Systems Corp.
1103 Maple Street
P.O. Box 1129
Bristol, IN 46507-1129
(888) 663–4897, (574) 848–0090;
fax: (574) 848–0205
www.modguys.com
Sales territory: IA, IL, IN, KY, MI, MO, OH

Pittsville Homes, Inc.
5094 Second Avenue South
P.O. Box C
Pittsville, WI 54466
(715) 884–2511; fax: (715) 884–2136
www.pittsvillehomes.com
Sales territory: WI

Pleasant St. Homes, LLC
Including Holly Park and Sun Building Systems
51700 Lovejoy Drive
Middlebury, IN 46540
(574) 825–3700; fax: (574) 825–3050
www.holly-park.com
Sales territory: IA, IL, IN, KY, MI, MN, MO, OH, WI, WV

Pleasant Valley Modular Homes, Inc.
100 Hammersmith Drive
P.O. Box 88
Pine Grove, PA 17963
(570) 345–8600; fax: (570) 345–4440
www.pvmhi.com
Sales territory: CT, DE, MA, MD, NH, NJ, NY, PA, RI, VA, VT, WV

Pro-Built Homes
20 Industrial Circle
Mifflintown, PA 17059
(866) 436–8677, (717) 836–6140;
fax: (717) 436–6481
www.pro-builthomes.com
Sales territory: CT, DE, MD, ME, NC, NH, NJ, NY, PA, RI, VA, VT, WV

Professional Building Systems Inc.
72 East Market Street
Middleburg, PA 17842
(570) 837–1424; fax: (570) 837–6133
www.pbsmodular.com
Sales territory: CT, DE, MA, MD, ME, NH, NJ, NY, OH, PA, RI, VA, VT, WV

Professional Building Systems of North Carolina, LLC
610 West Allenton Street
Mount Gilead, NC 27306
(800) 439–4317; fax: (910) 439–4558
www.pbsmodular.com
Sales territory: FL, GA, NC, OH, TN, VA, WV

R-Anell Housing Group LLC
3549 North Highway 16
P.O. Box 428
Denver, NC 28037
(704) 483–5511; fax: (704) 483–5674
www.r-anell.com
Sales territory: AL, FL, GA, NC, SC, TN, VA, WV

RCM Modular
28 Industrial Road
Beauce, QC G0M 1P0 Canada
(418) 227–4044; fax: (418) 227–3654
www.rcmmodulaire.com,
www.rcmmodular.com
Sales territory: Ontario, Quebec, CT, MA ME, NH, PA, VT

Ritz-Craft Corp.
15 Industrial Park Road
P.O. Box 70
Mifflinburg, PA 17844
(800) 326–9836; fax: (570) 966–9248
www.ritz-craft.com
Sales territory: CT, DE, GA, IA, IL, IN, KY, MA, MD, ME, MI, MO, NC, NH, NJ, NY, OH, PA, RI, SC, TN, UT, VA, WI, WV

❖ An increasing number of manufactured (or HUD-code) home manufacturers are adding modular home-building capabilities to their plants to offer home owners and builders more variety in their housing choices.

Rochester Homes Inc.
P.O. Box 587
Rochester, IN 46975
(800) 860–4554; fax: (574) 223–1655
www.rochesterhomesinc.com
Sales territory: IA, IL, IN, KY, MI, OH, WI

Samson Homes
1800 Northwestern Parkway
Louisville, KY 40203
(877) 353–7468, (502) 772–5280;
fax: (502) 774–5644
www.samsonhomes.com
Sales territory: IN, KY, OH, TN, WV

SEhomes, Inc.
Including Energy Homes, Southern Homes, Energy of Texas, and Southern Estates
P.O. Box 390
Addison, AL 35540
(256) 747–8589; fax: (256) 747–7586
www.sehomes.com
Sales territory: Southern United States, including Texas

Shamrock Homes
1201 West Markley Road
Plymouth, IN 46563
(574) 935–5111; fax: (574) 935–4015
www.shamrock-homes.com
Sales territory: IL, IN, MA, MI, MO, NJ, NY, OH, PA, RI, WI

Signature Building Systems Inc.
1004 Springbrook Avenue
Moosic, PA 18507
(570) 774–1000; fax: (570) 774–1010
www.signaturecustomhomes.com
Sales territory: CT, DE, FL, GA, MA, MD, ME, NC, NH, NJ, NY, PA, RI, SC, VA, VT, WV

Simplex Industries, Inc.
Keyser Valley Industrial Park
1 Simplex Drive
Scranton, PA 18504
(800) 233–4233, (570) 346–5113;
fax: (570) 346–3731
www.simplexind.com,
www.simplexhomes.com
Sales territory: CT, DC, DE, GA, MA, MD, ME, NC, NH, NJ, NY, PA, RI, SC, VA, VT, WV

Southern Structures
334 Cypress Road
Ocala, FL 34472
(352) 680–1911; fax: (352) 680–1903
www.southernstructuresinc.com
Sales territory: FL

Stratford Homes Ltd. Partnership
402 South Weber Avenue
P.O. Box 37
Stratford, WI 54484
(800) 488–1524, (715) 687–3133;
fax: (715) 687–3453
www.stratfordhomes.com
Sales territory: AK, CO, IA, ID, IL, KS, MI, MN, MO, MT, NE, OR, WA, WI

Sun Building Systems
Division of Pleasant St. Homes, LLC
9 Stauffer Industrial Park
Taylor, PA 18517
(570) 562–0110; fax: (570) 562–0737
www.sunmodular.com
Sales territory: New England, DE, MD, NJ, NY, PA, WV

❖ With a modular home, just like a HUD-code home, you (with your builder) are responsible for preparing the building site for the modules (such as the foundation) and completing their construction on-site.

Terrace Homes
1553 Eleventh Drive
Friendship, WI 53934
(608) 339–7888; fax: (608) 339–9361
www.terracehomes.com
Sales territory: IA, IL, MI, MN, WI

Timberland Homes
1201 Thirty-seventh Northwest
Auburn, WA 98001
(800) 488–5036, (253) 735–3435;
fax: (253) 939–8803
www.timberland-homes.com
Sales territory: AK, ID, OR, MT, WA

Unibilt Industries, Inc.
4671 Poplar Creek Road
P.O. Box 373
Vandalia, OH 45377
(800) 777–9942; fax (937) 890–8303
www.unibilt.com
Sales territory: IN, KY, OH, MI, WV

Vantage Pointe Homes, Inc.
1000 West Rokeby Road
Lincoln, NE 68523
(402) 423–8821; fax: (402) 423–8661
www.vpnebraska.com
Sales territory: KS, NE, SD

Virginia Homes Manufacturing Corp.
142 Virginia Homes Lane
P.O. Box 410
Boydton, VA 23917
(434) 738–6107; fax: (434) 738–6926
www.virginiahomesmfg.com
Sales territory: DE, MD, NC, NJ, PA, SC, VA

Wardcraft Homes, Inc.
1201 West Old 56 Highway
Olathe, KS 66061
(888) 927–3272; fax: (913) 390–1701
www.wardcraft.com
Sales territory: CO, KS, MO, NE, OK, SD, WY

Waterford Homes, LLC
947 Waterford Road
P.O. Box 206
Waterford, ME 04088
(207) 583–4100; fax: (207) 583–4900
www.waterfordhomesllc.com
Sales territory: ME

Wausau Homes, Inc.
P.O. Box 8005
Wausau, WI 54402-8005
(715) 359–7272; fax: (715) 359–5903
www.wausauhomes.com
Sales territory: FL, IA, IL, IN, MI, MN, OH, WI

**Westchester Modular
Homes, Inc.**
30 Reagans Mill Road
Wingdale, NY 12594
(800) 832–3888, (845) 832–9400;
fax; (845) 832–6698
www.westchester-modular.com
Sales territory: CT, MA, ME, NH, NJ,
NY, PA, RI, VT

Wisconsin Homes, Inc.
425 West McMillan
P.O. Box 250
Marshfield, WI 54449
(715) 384–2161; fax: (715) 387–3627
www.wisconsinhomesinc.com
Sales territory: IA, IL, MI, MN,
SD, WI

**Yellow Hammer Building
Systems**
Division of Cardinal Homes
2406 Highway 31 South
Bay Minette, AL 36507
(251) 937–1100; fax: (251) 937–0568
www.cardinalhomes.com/yellow
Sales territory: AL, FL, GA, MS

Trade Associations

Building Systems Councils

National Association of Home Builders (NAHB)

1201 Fifteenth Street NW

Washington, DC 20005

(800) 368–5242, ext. 8576

www.buildingsystems.org

The Building Systems Councils (BSC) represent the interests of concrete, log, modular, and panel (or panelized) home manufacturers, builders, and suppliers. The BSC's primary focus is to promote the benefits of systems-built housing. The Web site includes a thorough introduction of systems-built housing and the benefits of the technology, including a downloadable PowerPoint presentation; information about award-winning homes and member companies; details about the annual showcase trade show and conference; and various council membership directories. The BSC also publishes *Building Systems* magazine (www.buildingsystems.com); the magazine's Web site provides a list to current and past articles about the industry.

Manufactured Housing Institute

2101 Wilson Boulevard, Suite 610

Arlington, VA 22201-3062

(703) 558–0400; fax: (703) 558–0401

www.manufacturedhousing.org

The Manufactured Housing Institute (MHI) is the national trade organization representing all segments of the factory-built housing industry. MHI serves its membership of manufacturers, suppliers, and affiliates by providing industry research, promotion, education, and government relations programs, and by building and facilitating consensus within the industry. An online Consumer Center provides information about the history, definition, advantages of manufactured housing and the HUD code, including frequently asked questions, related links, and a membership directory by state, category, or company name.

Modular Building Systems Association

3029 North Front Street, Third Floor

Harrisburg, PA 17110

(717) 238–9130; fax: (717) 238–9156

www.modularhousing.com

The Modular Building Systems Association (MBSA) has represented the modular housing industry for more than thirty years, with members and affiliates throughout North America. Interested home buyers can use the MBSA as a resource for locating and contacting approved MBSA members and their affiliated builder/dealers to purchase a home. The Web site provides information about he modular building process and the benefits of the technology, as well as a directory of member companies by region and state.

National Modular Housing Council

2101 Wilson Boulevard, Suite 610

Arlington, VA 22201-3062

(703) 558–0400; fax: (703) 558–0401

www.modularcouncil.org (via www.manufacturedhousing.org)

The National Modular Housing Council (NMHC) provides modular manufacturers, suppliers, and builders with industry support and offers consumer links to members (via a regional/state directory), information, and related links.

HOUSING AFFORDABILITY WORKSHEET

Use this worksheet to record your expenses each month for three to six months and check off whether each expense is essential or nonessential. At the end of that time, record the *average* for each category on a blank version of the worksheet. Refer to your monthly worksheets to prioritize and determine whether each expense is essential or nonessential.

On another piece of paper, list your expenses in either essential or nonessential categories, then add up each category. Your nonessential spending list is what you've identified as "negotiable" to either eliminate or reduce to boost your housing affordability.

Month_____ **Year**_____

ESSENTIAL	NONESSENTIAL	EXPENSES	AMOUNT (monthly average)
☐	☐	**Mortgage** (including principal, interest, property taxes, insurance)	_____
		Utilities	
☐	☐	Natural gas/propane	_____
☐	☐	Electric	_____
☐	☐	Water/sewer	_____
☐	☐	Phone	_____
☐	☐	Trash/recycling	_____
☐	☐	Dial-up Internet/DSL	_____
☐	☐	Irrigation	_____
		Cable/satellite (incl. equipment)	_____
☐	☐	Television	_____
☐	☐	Internet	_____
		Insurance	_____
☐	☐	Health/medical	_____
☐	☐	Auto	_____
☐	☐	Life	_____
☐	☐	Home (unless part of mortgage)	_____
☐	☐	Other (specify)	_____
☐	☐	**Groceries/sundries**	_____
☐	☐	**Medical** (out of pocket)	_____
☐	☐	**Veterinary/pet care**	_____
☐	☐	**Vehicle payment(s)**	_____
☐	☐	**Boat/recreational vehicle payments**	_____
☐	☐	**Gasoline** (for vehicles)	_____
☐	☐	**Lawn service**	_____
☐	☐	**Health club dues/class fees**	_____
☐	☐	**Home improvement**	_____
☐	☐	**Self-/mini-storage**	_____
☐	☐	**Haircuts/health and beauty services**	_____
☐	☐	**Gifts**	_____
☐	☐	**Travel**	_____
☐	☐	**Entertainment**	_____
☐	☐	**Newspaper/media services**	_____
		Misc./other expenses (specify)	
☐	☐	_____	_____

NEEDS AND WANTS WORKSHEET

Use this worksheet to make decisions about what you must have and what you can live without (if perhaps only temporarily) in your new kit or manufactured home. It may help determine where you want to live and the availability of nearby services and amenities.

To get started, keep two lists: one labeled "Home" and another labeled "Activities." Focus the home list on ideas and features within and around your new home, including the number of bedrooms and bathrooms, the type of kitchen layout and finishes, a mud room, and similar details. Use the activities list to capture what you want to do in your home and in the location of your home, such as watch videos, play pool, swim (or other sports or recreation), and what access you want to civic, retail, and academic opportunities. Be as specific as possible.

Keep these lists handy or carry them with you. Add things as you think of them or see them while driving or walking through a neighborhood, visiting model homes, reading lifestyle magazines, or surfing the Internet. Give yourself at least a few weeks to create comprehensive home and activities lists.

Once you've exhausted your ideas, create separate lists of wants (nonessentials) and needs (essentials) for both your home and activities lists, then combine them under the "Wants" or "Needs" columns. Allow yourself time to mull over tough choices and assess your lifestyle habits to determine whether something—extra storage, a home office, nearby recreation, or close proximity to work, to name a few—is essential or not for the house you're planning to build or buy. There are no right or wrong answers; only you can determine and prioritize what's important to you and your family in a new home.

HOME	WANT	NEED	ACTIVITIES	WANT	NEED
_____	☐	☐	_____	☐	☐
_____	☐	☐	_____	☐	☐
_____	☐	☐	_____	☐	☐
_____	☐	☐	_____	☐	☐
_____	☐	☐	_____	☐	☐
_____	☐	☐	_____	☐	☐
_____	☐	☐	_____	☐	☐
_____	☐	☐	_____	☐	☐
_____	☐	☐	_____	☐	☐
_____	☐	☐	_____	☐	☐
_____	☐	☐	_____	☐	☐
_____	☐	☐	_____	☐	☐
_____	☐	☐	_____	☐	☐
_____	☐	☐	_____	☐	☐
_____	☐	☐	_____	☐	☐
_____	☐	☐	_____	☐	☐
_____	☐	☐	_____	☐	☐
_____	☐	☐	_____	☐	☐
_____	☐	☐	_____	☐	☐
_____	☐	☐	_____	☐	☐
_____	☐	☐	_____	☐	☐

ONGOING AND UP-FRONT COSTS WORKSHEET

Every home project has up-front and ongoing costs. It's important not only to identify and track these costs but also to separate them so you can anticipate what and when you'll be expected to pay for your new home and its operation and maintenance.

The following worksheet gets you started. It identifies costs as either up-front or ongoing expenses and enables you to fill in the amounts you can pay or have committed to pay as part of a loan or other agreement. Feel free to add or subtract costs as they relate to your specific circumstances.

UP-FRONT COSTS

Defined as one-time expenses

Land (if planning to pay cash): _____

Land development/improvements

    Utility services to site: _____

    Curb/gutter/driveway: _____

    Excavation/clearing: _____

    Other (specify): _____

Building permit and related development fees: _____

Design (e.g., changes to a stock house plan): _____

Construction: _____

Other (specify): _____

_____

_____

ONGOING COSTS

Defined as periodic (monthly, annual) expenses related to debt service and the maintenance and operation of your home while occupied

Mortgage payment/debt service (land loan, etc.): _____

Utilities: _____

Insurance: _____

Recreational/community association dues: _____

Maintenance/home improvements: _____

Home-related services (e.g., lawn care): _____

Other (specify): _____

_____

_____

_____

Glossary

Add-ons: Extras, often for an additional price.

Amenities: Activities or features (such as walking paths, tennis courts, pool) to which residents of a community or the surrounding area have access.

Amortized: Spread out over time.

Appreciated in value: Increased, as in the asking price or market value of a house.

Approvals: Consent by the appropriate building authority to issue a permit and begin construction once certain conditions (e.g., code-compliant building plans) are met.

As is: In current condition, with no changes.

Assessed value: The fair price or market value of a house based on a calculation of similar structures.

Baby boom generation: Roughly the generation of American citizens born between 1946 and 1964, representing about 80 million people.

Beams: Load-carrying, horizontal structural frame members.

Bid estimates, bids: Estimated costs for construction provided by builders or contractors.

Blueprints: The detailed plans used to gain approvals and for construction; also known as "working drawings" or "construction drawings."

Building envelope: A house that is "closed in" with its roofing, exterior siding, windows, and doors installed.

Building pad: An excavated home site ready for construction; also known as "pad."

Building permits: Documentation that confirms approval of construction.

Change orders: Requests by the home owner to alter the agreed plans or specifications.

Chassis: A metal frame with wheels and a tow bar upon which manufactured (HUD-code) homes are built, enabling them to be towed by big rig from the factory to the home site.

Concrete pad, concrete slab: A slab foundation or other monolithic concrete surface (such as a patio).

Construction drawings: The detailed plans or blueprints used by the builder and various contractors during construction; also known as "working drawings."

Construction manager: The person in charge of the job site during construction; also known as "site superintendent," "lead," or "CM."

Construction-to-permanent (C2P) loan: A loan in which the construction loan amount and terms are converted to a mortgage loan on the finished home and property.

Crane placement: The use of a crane to place or set panels or sections of a home on its foundation.

Customization: Altering a stock house plan to suit lifestyle or other needs.

Design criteria: A set of rules or specifications governing the design of a house.

Dimensional stability: The long-term ability of a structural framing member to remain straight and at its designed strength value.

Direct sales: Sales made to home owner-buyers directly instead of through a dealer network.

Dormer: A structure projecting from a sloped roof, usually with a window.

Draws: Scheduled payments.

Drywall: Sheets (or panels) of gypsum-based wallboard used instead of plaster to cover interior wall and ceiling framing members; also known as Sheetrock, a brand name of United States Gypsum.

Elevations: Two-dimensional renderings or representations of a vertical surface (such as a wall).

Energy Star: A federal program that sets standards for the energy use of a variety of consumer products (www.energystar.gov).

Engineered framing components: A generic term for roof trusses, wall and roof panels, and floor trusses, which are assembled/built in a factory and shipped to the job site to help speed on-site construction of major structural framing sections (e.g., the roof).

Entry porticos: A covered area projecting from the front door or porch/stoop, supported by columns.

Excavated, excavation: Clearing a raw parcel of land for construction; the removal of dirt for the construction of a foundation.

Explicit warranty: A printed or documented contract to fix legitimate problems within a certain time period.

Extended warranties: Contracts to service problems or defects beyond the standard terms.

Final assembly: The last bit of work required to complete a manufactured or modular home on the home site; also known as "final tie-ins."

Final inspection: The last scheduled inspection by a third party or independent building department official prior to move-in.

Final tie-ins: The last bit of work required to complete a manufactured or modular home on the home site; also known as "final assembly."

Floor plan: The interior layout of a house, usually shown in two-dimensional format from a bird's-eye view.

Floor trusses: Engineered, factory-built floor beams.

Footprint: The outline of a house's perimeter.

Forms: The molds in which concrete is poured to create walls, slabs, beams, and footings; also known as "formwork."

Headers: Structural framing members above an opening (e.g., door or window).

Higher-pitched roofs: Roof slopes greater than a 4-inch rise for every 12 inches in length.

Hinged (roof): A mechanism that enables higher-pitched roofs on manufactured houses.

Home equity: The difference between a home's market value and the current mortgage balance due.

House plan books: Printed catalogs of stock home plans.

HUD: The U.S. Department of Housing and Urban Development.

HUD code: The building codes and standards for manufactured homes established and enforced by the U.S. Department of Housing and Urban Development (HUD).

I joists: I-shaped engineered floor beams.

Infrastructure: Primarily refers to streets, curbs, gutters, storm-water runoff provisions, and other basic utility services necessary before construction begins.

In-house financing: Lending services or loans offered by the builder; also known as "private financing."

In-house mortgage entities: Mortgage lending services provided or offered by the builder or supplier.

Inspections: Periodically scheduled mandatory checks conducted by a third party to ensure a house is being built according to the approved plans and specifications.

Installed sales: When a supplier (e.g., lumberyard or home center) agrees or offers to install a product as a condition of the sale of that product.

Joists: Floor or roof beams.

Kit home: A package of building materials based on a selected floor plan and specifications from a single supplier or manufacturer.

Kit home package: An unassembled package of building materials, typically raw or precut lumber and other rough framing components, for a specific house plan selected by the home buyer, delivered to the job site for assembly.

Land-home package: A sale that includes both the house and the parcel of land on which it will be built or placed.

Lender: A bank or other financial institution that lends money.

Lien releases: Documents that prove all claims for labor and materials costs have been paid in full or to the supplier's satisfaction; also known as "lien waiver."

Linear massing: A long, flat elevation.

Log home: A kit or stick-built house constructed of (or to replicate) logs from cut trees.

Lump-sum payment: A debt or cost paid at one time instead of amortized over time.

Manufactured housing: General term for homes built in a factory to federal standards set by HUD.

Mechanical runs: The length of the wires, cables, ductwork, and plumbing pipes from their respective sources (e.g., the furnace) to various rooms in the house.

Mobilize: To get ready to build, specifically by moving tools, equipment, and materials to a job site prior to the start of construction.

Model building codes: Standards approved for adoption and enforcement by state or local building departments or authorities.

Model homes: Completed homes at a builder's sales center or subdivision used as a marketing device to sell more homes.

Modular: A type of factory-built construction in which sections of completed homes are assembled at the home site.

Modular homes: Homes primarily built in a factory in large sections, including rough mechanical systems but often lacking most finishes; assembled and finished on the job site.

Move-in: Occupancy.

Multiple-use rights: Authorization or restrictions regarding the use of a stock home plan more than one time.

Multisection: More than one section (e.g., "double-wide").

Nail pops: The heads of nails showing through a finished wall.

Offset sections: Sections of a manufactured house that are staggered to create dimension.

Off-site: Synonymous with manufactured or HUD-code homes; a home built primarily in a factory and shipped nearly complete to the job site.

On-site: Opposite of off-site; a home built primarily on the job site using raw or precut lumber and other materials needed for completion.

Options: Alternatives to what is standard or offered in the basic house at no additional charge.

Outbuildings: Separate or supplemental structures from the house or main building on the same property.

Pad: An excavated home site ready for construction; also known as "building pad."

Panelization: The use of factory-built structural framing components, including walls (or "panels"), roof trusses, and floor trusses.

Parcel: Land or home site.

Permits: Documents proving acceptance and payment for various stages of construction to commence, which are posted at the home site and referred to by building inspectors to confirm proper construction methods and materials.

Per-square-foot basis: A method for calculating costs based on a square foot of area; also known as "square-foot basis."

Piggyback (roof): A mechanism that enables higher-pitched roofs on manufactured houses.

Placed: A manufactured home craned into place on its foundation or pad at the home site; also known as "set."

Plated roof trusses: Factory-built roof framing components, in which steel plates hold sections of lumber together in a designed pattern or shape.

Plates: Horizontal wood framing members placed between the foundation and the wall framing.

Platform: A horizontal surface upon which to build walls.

Posts: Load-carrying, vertical structural frame members.

Pneumatic: Driven by compressed air.

Precut: Structural lumber and components that prior to delivery have been cut to length or to fit according to the plans and specifications.

Prefabricated: Made or built elsewhere, typically in a factory.

Prehung windows: Windows built with a frame and sill that are preassembled in a factory and installed as is during construction.

Prepriced: The price of an item as already determined.

Pressure-treated wood: Lumber or other wood building products that have been treated with a chemical to resist rot, decay, and insect infestation; used when the wood product touches the ground.

Private financing: Lending services or loans offered by the builder; also known as "in-house financing."

Production cycle: The time between excavation and move-in; the building process.

Punch list: Items left to complete.

Rafters: Structural members of the roof frame.

Raised-floor framing: A type of construction in which the first floor is built over a basement or crawl space.

Raw (land): Land that has yet to be prepared for building activity; pristine or unimproved.

Refinanced (loan): A loan for which the terms (interest rate, payment schedule) have been renegotiated.

Reverse plan: A mirror image of a house plan.

Review mechanisms (design): The process by which a design criteria is executed or enforced.

Roof ridge: The top of the roof along a horizontal plane.

Rough-in: The various wires, cables, pipes, and other "behind the wall" conduits that bring services from a source (e.g., the main electrical panel) to locations in the house.

Scope of work: Specific steps toward completion; the entire breadth of the project from start to finish.

Second-story platform: The "foundation" for a second story of a house.

Secured loans: Loans in which the amount is protected or balanced by collateral of equal or greater value.

Semicustom: A basic house plan or house features altered to accommodate lifestyle or other needs without sacrificing production efficiencies.

Service panel: A central location to which a utility (e.g., electricity) enters the house and is then distributed throughout the house.

Set: A manufactured home craned into place on its foundation or pad at the home site; also known as "placed."

Showrooms: Separate locations where a builder, dealer, or supplier may showcase available products, options, and upgrades.

Site-built: Houses built entirely on the home site (instead of in a factory).

Site improvements: Adding or bringing utility services to and creating a building area (or pad) on a parcel of raw land.

Skirting: A finish detail around the base of a manufactured (HUD-code) home that conceals the chassis.

Slab foundation: An at-grade, monolithic section of concrete that serves as the structural base of the house or other building.

Slope: The angle of the roof from its peak or ridge to the eaves.

Soil bearing capacity: The ability of the soil to withstand the weight of the finished house.

Soils tests: Tests to determine the composition of the soil upon which you want to build. The results may determine the type of foundation or other construction methods allowed or required.

Specifications: The written requirements for materials, equipment, construction systems, and standards.

Speculative model homes: Completed homes at a builder's sales center or subdivision used as a marketing device to sell more homes.

Square-foot basis: A method for calculating costs based on a square foot of area; also known as "per-square-foot basis."

Stick-built home: A house built using only uncut or precut structural lumber.

Stock home plans: Predesigned house plans.

Studs: Wall framing.

Study (or review) sets: Less-detailed sets of blueprints provided to a potential plan or home buyer for review purposes.

Swap in: Switch to an alternative, such as a different brand or style of sink or cabinets.

Tape and texture: The process for concealing the joints between sheets of gypsum wallboard (drywall) and applying a texture or pattern prior to paint or other wall finish.

Textured: Interior or exterior wall surfaces with an applied texture or pattern.

Title: Legal documents indicating the right of ownership to real property.

Timber frame: A type of construction using heavy-duty structural timbers in a post-and-beam configuration.

Turnkey: Start to finish, completely.

Undeveloped (land): Land that has been cleared or prepared for the installation of basic utility services prior to construction.

Upgrades: Items or features that are available for an additional cost beyond what is standard or offered in the basic house (e.g., whirlpool tub versus standard bathtub).

Utility extensions: Bringing utility services (e.g., water) from the main line in the street to the house.

Vellum: A house plan or construction document in reproducible format.

Volume: Ceiling heights that are higher than 8 feet.

Walk-throughs: Tours of a house under construction or recently completed.

Working drawings: The detailed plans or blueprints required for approvals or construction; also known as "construction drawings."

Zoning approval: Authorization to build a certain type of structure in a chosen area.

Recommended Reading

Gianino, Andrew. *The Modular Home.* Storey Publishing, 2005.

Grissim, John. *The Complete Buyer's Guide to Manufactured Homes and Land: How to Find a Reputable Dealer and Negotiate a Fair Price on the Best Kept Secret in American Housing.* Rainshadow Publications, 2003.

Heldmann, Carl. *How to Afford Your Own Log Home,* fifth edition. Globe Pequot Press, 2002.

Morris, Michael, and Dick Pirozzolo. *The Timberframe Way.* Lyons Press, 2003.

Smith, Carol. *Building Your Home: An Insider's Guide.* Home Builder Press of the National Association of Home Builders, 1996.

Stevenson, Katherine Cole, and H. Ward Jandl. *Houses by Mail: A Guide to Houses from Sears, Roebuck and Company.* John Wiley, 1995.

Thornton, Rosemary. *The Houses That Sears Built: Everything You Ever Wanted to Know about Sears Catalogue Homes.* Gentle Beam Publications, 2002.

Youssef, Wasfi, Ph.D. *Building Your Own Home: A Step-by-Step Guide.* John Wiley, 1988.

Index

Page numbers in **bold** refer to illustrations.

stock home plans. *See* house plans
structural insulated panels (SIPs), 66–67, **67**, 69, 73
study sets. *See* blueprints
subcontractors, 29, 32, 36, 44, 47, 50, 52, 74

T

three-bid rule, 47
Timberframe Way, The, xii
trade associations, 126
trade contractors. *See* subcontractors
tradespeople. *See* subcontractors
trailer coaches, **5,** 5–6, 7, 87, **87**

U

undeveloped land. *See* raw land
University of Missouri–Columbia, **6**
up-front costs, 27–28
U.S. Department of Housing and Urban Development, xii, 14, 91

V

vellum, 41, 72

W

walk-through inspection, 32, 52, 71
wall panels, 59, 62, 65
wants and needs worksheet
    blank, 128
    sample, 23
warranty, 73–74, 111–12
Wood Truss Council of America, 63
working drawings. *See* blueprints

Photo Credits

© AbleStock/IndexOpen: p. 29

Image courtesy of Alfred P. Sloan Museum: p. 4

© 1997–2006 American Standard Building Systems, Inc.: pp. viii third down on right, 81

© 2006 Rich Binsacca: pp. 8 top, 19 bottom, 24–25, 55, 56 top, 57 top, 61 top

Courtesy of BMC West: pp. 27, 36 top

Courtesy of BP America, Inc.—*Stanolind Record* (Standard Oil [Indiana] employee magazine, February 1920) picture of Sears homes in Wood River, Illinois; provided courtesy of Rose Thornton (www.searshomes.org), author of *The Houses That Sears Built,* and the Wood River Museum: p. 1

© Classic Post & Beam: pp. 11, 34 top

Clayton Homes, Inc.: p. 9 bottom

© 2005 Coachmen Industries, Inc.: p. 119

© EdgeBuilder Wall Panels/Woodmaster Foundations, Prescott, WI: pp. 20, 62

Courtesy of www.eplans.com © Hanley Wood, LLC: p. 39

© 1999 EyeWire, Inc. All rights reserved: pp. 19 top, 28, 58 top, 71, 74

Courtesy of FarWest Homes: pp. 34 bottom, 56 middle

© Fleetwood Enterprises, Inc.: p. 7

Courtesy of Guerdon Enterprises: pp. 93, 103 top, 103 bottom, 104 middle, 104 bottom, 105 bottom, 106

Courtesy of HandCrafted Homes, Henderson, NC: xi, 86, 5 top, 97 middle, 97 bottom

© HandCrafted Homes, LLC: p. 121 top

© Harvest Homes Panelized Building System: pp. 10 top, 68, 82

© Haven Homes, Beech Creek, PA: pp. viii bottom, 121 bottom

© Hayward Lumber: pp. 44, 63, 64

© Hive Modular: pp. 36 bottom, 83 left

© HomeBuilder.com: p. 48

Reprinted with permission from www.homebuilders.org produced by the Home

Builders Association of Maryland. All rights reserved: pp. 49 top, 49 bottom

Portions of this publication reproduce the cover image from the 2006 *International Residential Code®* For One- and Two-Family Dwellings, International Code Council, Inc., Falls Church, Virginia. Reproduced with Permission. All Rights Reserved: p. 46

© Keith Levit Photography/IndexOpen: p. 16

© LLC, FogStock/IndexOpen: pp. xii, 51

© Manufactured Housing Institute: pp. viii middle right (truck), 5 bottom, 8 bottom, 9 top, 87–89, 90, 92, 97 top, 98, 100, 103 middle, 104 top, 105 middle, 107 middle, 107 bottom, 108, 122

Courtesy of Marmol Radziner Prefab © Benny Chan/fotoworks: pp. 65, 75, 83 right top

© 2004 Jason Munroe: p. 61 bottom

© Natural Spaces Domes: p. 83 bottom right

© Norse Building Systems, Inc., Ladysmith, WI: pp. viii top left, viii middle left, 38

© photolibrary.com pty, ltd./IndexOpen: p. 43

© Photos.com: p. 13

© R-Anell Homes: p. 107 top

© Riverbend Timber Framing: p. 34 middle

Courtesy of SEARS® (a registered trademark of Sears Brands, LLC): pp. x, 2

Courtesy of Structural Insulated Panel Association (SIPA): pp. 66, 67 top

C:1/81/1 Box 6 FF 92, Courtesy of University Archives, University of Missouri at Columbia: p. 6

Courtesy of Steve Welsh: pp. 10 bottom, 33, 60

© James F. Wilson: pp. 56 bottom, 57 middle, 57 bottom, 58 middle, 58 bottom, 59 top, 67 bottom

About the Author

Rich Binsacca is an award-winning journalist and author. *Kit Homes* is his fifteenth book on housing and related subjects. He has written and edited thousands of articles for trade, business, design, and lifestyle magazines and online publications. He is a graduate of the University of Missouri–Columbia School of Journalism and currently resides in Boise, Idaho, with his wife, two sons, and a cat.